SKINS of COLUMBUS

A DREAM ETHNOGRAPHY

Published in the United States by

Fence Books
110 Union Street
Second Floor
Hudson NY 12534

www.fenceportal.org

This book was designed by Rebecca Wolff
printed by Versa Press
and distributed by Small Press Distribution
and Consortium Book Sales and Distribution.

Library of Congress Control Number: 2019936244

Garcia, Edgar (1983-)
Skins of Columbus: A Dream Ethnography / Edgar Garcia

ISBN 13: 978-1-944380-10-6

First Edition
10 9 8 7 6 5 4 3

SKINS of COLUMBUS
A DREAM ETHNOGRAPHY

EDGAR GARCIA

FENCE MODERN POETS SERIES

This book is for Alexis, Inez, and Emma,
the real residents of my land of dreams

TABLE OF CONTENTS

Colonoscopy *1*

Journaling *4*

University Head *11*

Journaling *15*

Nahualli Without Organs *17*

Journaling *21*

Ohmaxac Packs (Tomorrow's Savages) *33*

Journaling *40*

Diary in the Strict Sense *45*

Journaling *46*

Bowl-Maker *58*

Journaling *63*

Diary in the Strict Sense *70*

Journaling *71*

Diary in the Strict Sense *78*

Journaling *79*

Notes by Page Number *i*

Oneirography *xvii*

Acknowledgments *xxiii*

The history of the dream remains to be written, and opening up a perspective on this subject would mean decisively overcoming the superstitious belief in natural necessity by means of historical illumination. Dreaming has a share in history.

WALTER BENJAMIN
"Dream Kitsch"

The conversation turned on questions of methodology of history... My attempt to explain a theory of history in which the concept of development is entirely supplanted by the concept of origins. Understood in this way, history cannot be sought in the riverbed of a process of development. Instead, as I have remarked elsewhere, the image of a riverbed is replaced by that of a whirlpool. In such a whirlpool earlier and later events—the prehistory and posthistory of an event, or, better, of a status, swirl around it. The actual objects of a such a view of history are not specific events but specific unchanging statuses of a conceptual or sensual kind—for example, the Russian agrarian system, the city of Barcelona, population shifts in the Mark of Brandenburg, barrel vaulting, and so on.

WALTER BENJAMIN
"Diary from Aug 7, 1931, to the Day of My Death"

History is the observation of facts in keeping with a certain theory; an application of this theory to the facts as time gives birth to them.—The life that lies behind me is opalescent, a shimmer of many colors. Some things strike and attract me. Others are dead.

BRONISLAW MALINOWSKI
A Diary in the Strict Sense of the Term

In the evening I read *Conquest of Mexico*. Fell asleep quickly. Strange dreams.

BRONISLAW MALINOWSKI
A Diary in the Strict Sense of the Term

The journal dreamt itself. Its pages you wrote to capture mental colony from its root in the name, Cristóbal Colón. But what captivities does the name, that sound—*Colón*—hide? Drop its diacritic and you drift like plastic in a sea of erotogenic marks. How does the large intestine entwine in the same sign that names the colon: punctuation preceding explanation, dramatizing the experience of figures and forms? What does a colon do, actually? To explain: what follows is a book whose poems examine the inner workings of colonial myth. To explore the burrowing of our colonial myths into real-life experience—wet violence in the tough skin of emblems and instincts—the author spent four months reading the journal of Christopher Columbus before sleep. Later, he transformed his dreams into a poetic record of what his memory, in its half-sleep, had forgotten it remembered: the gash, shock, glamour, void, punctuation, and spell of origins. It belonged to that history as intimately as that history belonged to the momentary constellations of a night sky. Its belonging, unclear and unassimilated, anacoluthic but self-instructive, is the shining of dark stars equipped with consciousness.

To say simply that you could subvert Columbus and the world he left us only stages the inadequacy of the curse to do away with the accursed object. As usual, reality is contrary. The curse imprecates the curser, the interdict awakens the nightmare, iconoclasts are slaves of icons, and, critical truisms though these may be, you conjure yourself inside them constantly: to subvert is to crumble to the enterprise of memory overturned, to hurl body over the head of mental colony only to flip back upward, part to an assed whole. So the question, for you at least, is how to flip from realities different than those of the colonial myth—how to stay true to the reality of myth, which bakes the crust of your thought with its hot white light, while hitching somehow to new suns and ideas. How do you look inside yourself for its terrible illumination while shedding new light on that light? Could you, with mirror or sword-face even for an instant, blind the gods and their higher powers?

To be clear: you are not looking for wisdom, but for a world unfolding in dreams. In October 2015, soon after moving to Chicago, you came up with a strategy for this. You came to it while browsing the yearly Hyde Park Used Book Sale, which takes place on Columbus Day weekend. In the chaotic pile of 30,000 books separated into 50 sections in Dole, Del Monte, and Chiquita produce boxes—emanations of the United Fruit Company—you came across a hardcover edition of Bartolomé de las

Casas's sixteenth-century *Journal of Christopher Columbus*. Reading the entry for that day, the 10th, there amid the boxes and browsing shoppers, you saw the rain chop the waves, shake the whole history from inside out, and take you into the storm pulling his ship down the sea. In two days, he would see land. But, at that moment, he was in the darkest kind of sleep. So you decided to awaken with him, to see if you could see what your mind saw in what he saw and, in doing so, to flash a mirror into the beach-boiled eye of the unsleeping colonial sun.

That night, and every night for the next three months during which he traveled the coasts, tricking history into his tasks, you read the journal before bed closely to have your sleeping mind think intently on its images, plots, symbols, motives, and feelings. You wished to see what, when left to its matrix of associations, your mind made of the colonial story. Notes throughout the night recorded your dreams. In the mornings, you made new notations to chart closer contacts between you two, dreamer and traveler. You composed the text in the evenings, putting your dreams and the journal together into a new story of creation. What you made you now hold in your hands: the positions, spaces, and temporalities of history are tasks you gave yourself, entanglements warped in a historical structure that depends on you for its unfolding churn, which discloses itself in both nights and days. Here is a study about how language is captivated by and captures the negativity of the hemispheric experience surging from its southern sources—how its inconsistency and unevenness are stopgaps because in practice a body and its myth are not exclusive of each other, but reciprocal and dynamic, semiotic and aesthetic. These are signs and the instances in which they unravel themselves. Like a first being looking out from the gauzy green light of a newborn cosmos, you saw the gods then as so many cascading storms.

EL TERZERO CAPITAN
CVCIVANCHIRE

Sunday∿Thursday, October 11

Roughest sea so far tube-nosed seabirds
on green reeds a cane a stick bobbing
carved iron and a small board with marks
like lizard hands
like little lights at the end of a hall
signaling pigs to squeal hopes of land

through day we landed and saw
the lizards upright like sideways
Fs or Ys upside-down
crimping their necks to look at us
impossible words by force by
fish chopping the water around us all

My Christ, my surrendering fish
I see what you signal:
To take the dinosaurs by force

Tuesday∿Saturday, October 13

To a broken planet came men
bellies and long hair, carved like
spears all wet all playing games

They are a pleasure to watch
so flat so slender so fast they

split my world in two into
a dead body hiding in my skin

Wednesday∿Sunday, October 14

The island sick fearful shouts to us
coming from heaven for help to us

Thursday⌇⌇Monday, October 15

Anchor daylight free from shoals
Hoisted sails, bracelets, legs, and arms
Crystals the shape of diamonds
I touched to make them shudder &
look away & I could take what I want

bracelets on their arms and legs
in their ears noses
and around their necks plus
some dry sliced leaves they prize

Friday & Saturday⌇⌇Tuesday & Wednesday, October 16

watching an airplane crash feels like
Is like what I feel watching their canoes
off the coast subtending
Making wobbly half-circles inside me
Bags of human shit hanging from my lungs
I don't know how to describe it
The explosive fire across the water
Have you ever seen a plane crash?
I haven't. But I fear what it feels like
Seeing all those people dip down

Saturday∿ᴝWednesday, October 17

Not all people are real; some races
missing eyes, missing circles

The real people of dreams w circles
in their eyes from the walk through
widening circles to fall asleep
circles that widen from their pupils
each of whose edges w many points
each of which is the center
of another widening w edges
are so many centers w the others
Like Emerson explained
But it's not a numbering not clean
It's a cloud thickening, thick with rain
that eventually you go right through
wet with eyes in the world of dreams

It has rained every day, more or less,
Since we have been in the Indies

Sunday∿ᴝThursday, October 18

Weather cleared we sailed around
stiff, impatient

Monday∿ᴝFriday, October 19

dawn orders midday sleeping so I did so
the men told me from the island I named
they could smell herbs, spices, dyes
whiffing like dogs with noses twitching
and nothing to do

TUESDAY∿Ʊ∩SATURDAY, OCTOBER 20

Nobody to talk to I met the king
his strange body   shallow water
the outer rims of his eyes
like rings which—slipped
over my fingers—the water
rippled I didn't want it to do that

WEDNESDAY∿Ʊ∩SUNDAY, OCTOBER 21

touched, lovely, green, fertile lagoons
flocks of parrots right in the sun

We killed some of them and kept
the feathers with the aloe and quintal
beads and kilograms of gold; the
birds rattled new songs in the jars

THURSDAY∿ᴗᴖMONDAY, OCTOBER 22

Head is so many
Many of which move up and down
a spiral staircase, at the bottom
level of which lives trauma

In there people, some naked
some painted, throw objects at an incinerator:
Abuse events, violence events
in there red white hot, heating
the whole black machine orange

Up the spiral staircase so many
made objects a workshop
bits of glass, pieced-together
cups, figurines, earthenware

Above that my business offices
junk furniture and dusty items

FRIDAY∿ᴗᴖTUESDAY, OCTOBER 23

I dream that I am in the 1980s
riding around in the back of a van
my uncle's van, the van
he bought from a cleaning company
whose name is painted on the side,
a cleaning company closed down

cannot tell you if I should feel bad
about it, an enterprise failed

Yours is a strange dream,
a strange reverie
CLAUDIA RANKINE, *Citizen*

At the end of June 2010, shortly before taking qualifying exams for graduate study, you travel to Guatemala City to see whether the particular difficulty of your life has any meaning in the company of extended family. Your cousin has invited you to visit him and his cat in their home in one of the southeastern colonias. It is the start of the rainy season, so you time your daily weave across the city to avoid the storms rolling through in the afternoon and evening. On one of your outings you visit the national university, fourth oldest in the Americas, where you snap a picture of the provost's office from across a greenish gauze of wet tropical trees and shrubbery. Lacking the uninterrupted confidence of a picture, a diary is anxious about its ability to seize the scene, scratching desperately for its trace. It worries its marks with the personal moods, papers, pleated rocks, and airs of the day.

The history of Columbus's journal is awkward. The extant version is a précis—evidently faithful (excluding navigational minutiae), made by de las Casas—that incorporates first-person narrative quotes from a copy of the original log. Its shaky Spanish reflects de las Casas' editorial commitment to originary dialectic, that is, either the Genoan's in a language foreign to him, or a semi-literate scribe's doing his best to copy. Garbled tones also complicate who comes first. Columbus writes to satisfy and elicit royal investments (so invites comparison of his journey to Marco Polo's); de las Casas writes a history, and decidedly one to disentangle these dreams from the vanity of human enterprise ("the vision of dreams is this against that, the likeness of a face confronting a face," reads his holy book, "do not give your mind to them. For dreams have deceived many, and those who put their hopes in them have failed"). Damned, then, is the book from the outset; damned, because it is a diary in search of pasts undreamt, a trace without interior. "Damned," in the words of Aimé Césaire, "because of the caravan of far-off interiors… Damned in the wake of world discoverers. Damned, because in the ears of the poet is re-attempted the same voice which haunted Columbus: 'I will found a new heaven and a new earth so wonderful that one will no longer think of who is to be first.'"

I don't keep a diary. But, if I did, I think that what I would have written at that time about that moment looking across the quad at the Universidad de San Carlos de Guatemala would have been thick with the obvious. Founded, like other colonial universities, as a nest in which to hatch the doctrine of the cross and sword, by the twentieth century the campus was a natural environment for the violent conflict between popular socialist movements and the military juntas allied with American fruit companies. Nearby is buried the body of a K'iche' peasant who one day in 1980 protested the decades-long depredation of the Guatemalan Civil War. That night, he was burned, revived, kidnapped, tortured, and hurled from the balustrade of the university president's mansion. Occult little spot of land, learning, war, and terror, the campus gives no immediate impression that anyone has ever died there.

Your cousin is placid about it all. Even though the publicized killing of your shared first cousin once removed—while commanding a squadron of FAR, the Rebel Armed Forces—forced your family to flee to Mexico, the United States, and Cuba, he tells you over drinks that things were bad then, sure, but not as bad as they are now. The wars for control of the fruit trade were nothing compared to those for control of the cocaine routes. In the banana republic there was a semblance of a republic, spellbound and crudely revelatory. He says the ability to see people vanishes now, to see enemies in their paralyzing light and friends without the mask of tiring violence.

After the war ended, malcontent soldiers, death squads, and secret police slipped into the vast criminal enterprise that is the state, small parts playing the roles of wholes in a gruesome theatrical bureaucracy that serves the trafficking of drugs, arms, and workable bodies. So eviscerated is the civic apparatus today that citizens hire assassins and form lynch mobs to secure justice. While the country doesn't have as high of a murder rate as other murder capitals of the world (every year more people are killed per capita in Baltimore or St. Louis, let alone San Salvador or Caracas), it is one of the *best places* in the world to kill: "ninety seven per cent of homicides remain unsolved," one investigative journalist writes, quoting a U.N. official, "Guatemala is a good place to commit a murder, because you will almost certainly get away with it."

From this vantage, the distant violence of the conquistadors is kin, complete, condensed, yet retrograde. You finish your drinks and cruise the Avenida las Americas where you pass the city's bronze statue of Columbus. Devoid of subtlety, he perches on a globe wrapped in the Spanish coat of arms, carried by African and Indian slaves. Time amasses in such objects. Not historical time, with its forward momentum leading inescapably to some other damned soul's murder in the country's vast spinning capital. Rather, time itself, in the crisis of its inequality, provokes a reckoning. All of those bodies, figures, monuments, machines, and avenues, "this against that," are incommensurate with one another, each one carrying its own way of organizing the experience of temporal restlessness, many pasts and futures vying to condition a living present, to guide its feelings and thoughts, each one playing thus the role of a whole in a holy theatre of ever-fragmenting parts. Each part is complete with the possibility of playing the whole, making the stage ungovernable, disunited, inconsistent, many and uneven, but not unlike so many migrants carrying discrepant, irreparable, real worlds of time in their creviced shoulders. This temporal heterogeneity involves not only what you call history, but also the cool ambiguous devils and combustible angels of catachrestic pasts. They intercalate, the other captures the imagination of the one, and the totalizable fragment breaks loose.

Five years earlier, newly graduated from college, you wrote a long poem to chip away at the tyranny of rectilinear time, the longest chain of the conquest. What you called your "mytho-economic epic of the Americas" wished to investigate how the lifeblood of those wars flows, like a myth or concept of time, in the everyday pulsing of one's veins. In one bit of it you spoke to Simón Bolívar—liberator of Venezuela, Bolivia, Columbia, Ecuador, Peru, and Panama—about the strange gods that preside over the violence of the continent's Olympus:

In the tropical climates of Cuscatlan and Goathemala the sun at midday appears to draw the clouds around itself in serpentine designs, and from these signed snakes come the thunder, lightning, and rain and here I sat with Bolivar, Lord of the Face of Torches, who said to me:

And we also have a dirty god about whom I could say nothing that isn't true; he lies, cheats, and steals; and when we met he was so faraway from everything I'd known I've probably hated him as much as I love him.

His skin is charred white from constant exposure to the sun; well traveled, his toothless gums protect those who foolishly wander into unknown wastes.

In the next section of the poem you wander through a smoking hole in the jungle to the underworld, where you speak to underbelly gods paranoid about their ever-slipping control of the persistent now. One god you meet is Camazotz, Lord of the House of Death Bats, who says, "whoever fights a revolution ploughs the sea." His words are spoken to be unclear as to whether he sees himself as ocean or ploughman. Later, listening together to the sound of the sky between its cracking rains, he tells you about his exploits in the Guatemalan earthquake of Christmas 1917—his smile is emerald green in the smoky cellar light—when he covered the moon with a cloud of black wings to steal the head of the statue of bronze Columbus. This actually happened.

But the people had chosen their god. After the quake, the Genoan's head was recovered and reattached. And who today knows Camazotz? If you look close, though, you will notice the sutured statue's neck in Guatemala City. The crack that encircles his throat is the ocean of myth that encloses this American Hercules, as de las Casas called him, baffled at how many people the hero killed on a single island between 1494 and 1508. An Olympian proportion: "over three million from war, slavery, and the mines. Who in future generations will believe this? I myself writing as a knowledgeable eyewitness can hardly believe it."

SATURDAY∿∾WEDNESDAY, OCTOBER 24

I dream that I am in the 1980s again
in Japan in a museum

and my boat is there, its wood
creaks across my feet patchy
static atmospheres

I notice I was never in Japan
I am inside a television and someone else
is playing my part on TV

After the sun an octagonal Nine
south-west navigation
Eight nine times from within
each one Five leagues
or the length of a cathedral

We saw land again
all sad, all chest-like, all bruised
by rain

Difficult births.   [Rain, rain. On the vessel she outlines.]   Heat & (4) movement(s).

[White bloodclot.]   Pot of lime water, soaked corn.   [She, split in two.]

Dreams erupt in the face of great peril.
MICHAEL TAUSSIG, *The Magic of the State*

Visit any museum of anthropology in Mexico or Central America and you will notice that things come in pairs. On the same trip when I visited Guatemala City I went to see family outside San Salvador, in the municipality of Apopa. My mother's mother originated in coastal northwest Nicaragua, where she and her sister ferried goods in the Gulf of Fonseca between Potosí and La Union. Fabrics, jewelry, small food items, and household trinkets were their livelihood until the US occupation of Nicaragua restricted movement to and from the country. Rather than return to a hopeless war, the sisters settled in La Union, where my grandmother Amanda made her family. A feeling that I should talk to her about these things had inspired my trip, because that summer she was dying of leukemia. So we spent mornings, when she had a good energy for conversation, speaking on the concrete patio before the afternoon rains rolled in.

My plan was to spend the afternoons riding the roaring multicolored buses into nearby San Salvador to visit various sites. But my family would not allow it. It was far too dangerous in their town, they said, let alone in the ten mile stretch between it and the main city. Recently on that route, a gang had torched a bus full of passengers, shooting those who ran. The gangs expect the owners of these private buses to pay tribute to them and, when they don't, the maras do not hesitate to prove their seriousness. The biggest gang in El Salvador is a US export, Mara Salvatrucha or MS-13, which formed in the 1970s in Los Angeles as a cohort of stoner teenager Salvadoran fans of Slayer, Metallica, Megadeth, and Iron Maiden. Their metamorphosis originated in the surged circulation of crack cocaine in the early 1980s. Crack was at the height of its power, its foot soldiers rushing it to the poor, and groups like the Salvadoran stoners were simply left to their fate without any real chance of preventing its catastrophe. By the end of the decade, they were a solid prison gang, mercilessly violent and cruelly vengeful. Deported convicts took the brand back to Central America. Of its estimated 40–50,000 members, only one fifth reside in the US.

So my cousin said that we would drive together to the sites, along with her six-year old daughter. The main place that I wanted to visit was the museum of anthropology on the far west of the city, across several tense areas. This cousin and I had been close as children, as a consequence of near age. We had shared a frightening episode in 1986, when my mother took me with her to El Salvador to attend her brother's funeral. This was the time of the Salvadoran Civil War, and she was out one night doing something or other, when the left-wing guerrillas came to my grandmother's house in search of provisions. My cousin and I hid in a dresser while the adults negotiated the danger of abetting enemies of the state. Shortly after they left, that danger was realized when a group of soldiers arrived in search of the guerrillas. Again, we children hid. My cousin remembers playing in her mind a game of silence and hiding, in spite of the peril. I don't remember the incident at all. But the way in which her daughter looks and speaks exactly as she did then takes me back to that moment, captivated by the gross horror that little children are able to bear and the ignorant dignity with which they do so.

The museum is largely dedicated to the prehispanic culture of the Pipil people that once inhabited the western side of the country. Their language is related to Nahuatl of Central Mexico, and their mythology mirrors that of Aztecs and Mayans. This mythology makes its way into the folklore that my little cousin once removed learns in school. She tells me about Cipitio, the ash-eating child of the woods who is a version of Xipe Totec, the flayed Aztec god of war and regeneration; his mother, la Siguanaba, whose betrayal of Tlaloc, the Mesoamerican rain god, condemned her to haunt riversides and lakes; and the cadejos or magical deer-hooved dogs—the black one stands upright to let you know that it will harm you, while the white one will protect and help you. This is not exactly the difference between evil and good. Sometimes the attributes are reversed, so the black dog helps and the white harms. Their intentions are also complicated by the physical state of the person who finds them. They are each inclined to help drunks and desperate vagrants. Yet, conversely, anyone who turns their back on them or tries to speak to one of them will go insane. That is, unless the person is already insane, in which case conversation with the dogs can be beneficial. Moreover, the magical dogs can mate with regular dogs to produce a mutt who terrorizes but can never kill. It is even said that the black and white cadejos were human brothers whom a cruel sorcerer cursed, so that when they returned to their town transformed they were shunned and condemned to roam the countryside in search of the maledicting sorcerer.

Pairs of beings like the cadejos—who are mutually emergent, interdependent, and even interchangeable—are prototypical to the native mythologies of Central America and Mexico. The core beings of these mythological systems carry complementary contradictions: Feathered Serpent, Smoking Mirror, Burnt Water, Flowering War, and the Flayed God are the prominent representations of partnered aspects that do not synthesize, but instead remain in constant dis-identification, each lurking in the disclosures of the other. One of my favorite lines of Mayan poetry—spoken by Andres Xiloj Peruch, a Mayan daykeeper or diviner—is a description of dreams that calls on this idea: "it shines, it shimmers, in the blackness, in the night." It is in the blackness of night that the light of a dream shines; the visibility of its light depends on darkness, darkness that in turn depends on the light to draw out its significations from a void. Dreams and darkness hold each other in Mesoamerican space-time like the intersecting warp and weft in a weaving, as anthropologists Dennis and Barbara Tedlock (who transcribed Xiloj Peruch's words) describe. The metaphor of weaving bears a great deal of explanatory power: in as much as movement on any thread in a weaving affects its intersecting strands, each is understood to be in "complementary rather than opposed" relation to its other, the two "interpenetrating rather than mutually exclusive." As James Maffie, another anthropologist, also a philosopher, puts it, they are mutually emergent partners that "define, complement, [and] condition" each other. And such endless identity in impossible identification serves to affirm constant interchange that carries meanings of "self-emerging and self-transforming" form. The destiny of the cadejos to travel together tossing back-and-forth into each other without end is secretly ours as well. Our fate is to wander like deer-hooved dogs in hopeless search of originary maledictions.

The distance in time that separates the era of the Flayed God from that of Cipitio is a constant temporal condition of colonized people, is the embodiment of distances, is the intimacy of time's breaks, where the deer-hooved dogs push through their ensorcelled snouts, make explicit their consciousness of contradiction, and thus declaim themselves fleshy theory in technique, configuration as such. There is no going back, only to mark out those instances in which the times do not cohere, errors and wrecks marbled like crystal into earth-bed, when a little bird flies into the room to remind you of the geothermic tension between temporalities that is, under your slipping hooves, the field of political and social possibility—quick stillness that "can turn the self into a dreaming scene, if only for a minute," to quote one more anthropologist, Kathleen Stewart (19). Cadejos are the dreaming scene of heteroclite hiatus.

Beginning in January 2012, I collaborated on a blog with Jose-Luis Moctezuma, the author of the poem that is superimposed on the above picture of the stele. In this *blog*—a word whose unsightliness is adequate to the dialogue from which the project emerged, a dialogue stretching back to when we were teenagers—we gave up the search for curses without origin and origins too tired to be cursed. We embraced the dogged danger of transformation, and called this project by the Nahuatl word "nahualli" or shapeshifter, and we thought of it as a type of ritual collecting, documenting the many traces of self-splitting, cosmic pairing, and metamorphosis in the Americas that we came across: "a chattering seed grows suddenly to a green stalk," I wrote then, "while a mountain teems to personhood; and we match that overflow with overflow. Thus do we redistribute cosmic energy. Its first transfer long preceded our arrival; but we continue the exchange, the extension that is likewise our rootedness. To a great extent, this is simply the record of the personal reading habits of its co-curators."

One of the images that I posted to the blog is a photograph with which I left El Salvador. In this picture, my grandmother and her sister balance on a log with their arms stretched over the waters of their Gulf of Fonseca. Their antics mesmerize a group of swimmers beneath. What mesmerizes me about this picture is that it exists at all. Who in that rural poverty had a camera and why—besides the pull of these women's bodies on the threads of cosmic intersections—would a person take this picture? A nagualist attitude or theory of the cadejo moved furtively in the photographer's heart. I superimposed a poem on it to disclose these secret leanings.

May I be able to walk alongside you

May I be able to take you
a little puma claws the wood above me
May I be able to leave you

because I cannot think, this way or
and the little puma circled down like a
leap except on a heap of ashes
helecoid onto the worm's head

May I be able to follow you
May I be able to walk alongside you
May I be able to take you
May I be able to leave you

and the little puma circled down like a leaf
helecoid onto the worm's head

To choose as by something dividing the river's edge were
the dynamics of some thing becoming itself
bent or broken branches where the trees roots are

I be able to walk alongside you

I be able to take you
s the wood above me
I be able to leave you

think, this way or
he little puma circled down like a leaf
of ashes
onto the worm's head

follow you

walk alongside you

take you

leave you

circled down like a leaf

worm's head

something divided were

one thing becoming itself

where the tree's roots are a worm's open mouth

TUESDAY∿∿SATURDAY, OCTOBER 27

It wasn't until It was Into my hand
my strength Myself so lovely
that I noticed I wanted to kill them

holding it back like a bird in amaranth

free lonely river along coast shoals
Deep and clear and wide
But different from ours
Earlier somehow
Crudely abundant along coast shoals
Up to sunset-heavy rains

Thursday⌇⌇Monday, October 29

speech-like movements of leg and hip
As if they could understand something
In those things, everything they do

we knew and put them in military camps

We know how they watch us and wish
To touch us to them our wild birds
Our desire to kill in its outfits of net

We know we are fish and large and lovely
And trees and fruit and wonderful taste

And cows and herds is what they think our skulls
do all night Scented, sweet, involuted
with the salt In our mouths are
To kiss us To attribute the heat of these islands
to us To blow so warm with good landmark
and be calm as the rivers of Seville

Those people are like a mosque
Or mountain peak, projecting skyward
So badly they want to be with us

FRIDAY∿∾TUESDAY, OCTOBER 30

From the head
of the extensive mainland's
electromagnetic pulse
sat down the Grand Khan
the Tarot with him
And pulled the Universe

The rain outside the bungalow
lumbered into the thirsty sea

each drop an exterior
Suddenly inside something else
something much bigger

But thirsty nonetheless

The two ovals on the Khan's head
were so calm, so completely fixed
I couldn't say they were eyes

SATURDAY∿∾WEDNESDAY, OCTOBER 31

not being able
to enter the Great
City India whose
shallow inlets
let in only canoes
he returned wind
and went home

an unconcerned Khan

Sunday∿∾Thursday, November 1

Boats housed in usual pregnant time
appeared ordered everyone waiting
but the harm already had been tenant
a man walking among good people
with so many superimpositions, lying
you might say, but you might also say
simple—just looking for gold and silver.
Don't mind me, fellow Christians.

Tuesday∿∾Saturday, November 3

Shake hands terrorism who claws
Into my hand   which pushes
Back up but he keeps clawing down
Tells me never to forget terrorism
I realize   a lion, a less-than-human
We go   we exit the room running
Through a zoo-long hallway limbering
into lion's gait into an auditorium
where I the lion in a crowd of people
black out amazed by my rage to wreak
havoc they attack me—briefly giant
                              then dead.

Wednesday∿∾Sunday, November 4

Soccer fans swarmed the hive

Fear I am running away from control
Society avoiding police and what's
The word for surveillance by the
State and military coup personified

He says an Indian told him by signs
That mastic was good for tempering
stomach pains
and learning who wants to kill you

Yesterday, in the night
Two men sent into the interior came back
And they said where were one thousand
Large tents that received them
solemnity touching their sands
From Heaven to eat and understand
The most honorable kissing
Fondling and cinnamon and pepper

The ones that came back with them
Thought they were going to heaven
Ashore with partridges
Nightingales and abundant Indian corn

They are naked and when they look
At us we are naked beneath our clothes

Saturday∿〰Wednesday, November 7

Electromagnetic pulsation
from my mind
pushing out into cosmos

Drawing the Tarot
at the far end of
The Universe   Lakeshore Bike Ride
                  Raining outside

Entering celestial
orbs where outside

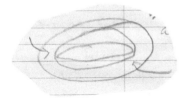

               gets in
               and inside
               out

sat. Nov 7

Electromagn. pulsations
from my mind
pushing out into cosmos

Drawing the Tarot
at far end of
Caketone Bike Ride
the owner parking outside

Enters celestial
orbs where ate
becomes thing
and lines
often

SUNDAY∿∿THURSDAY, NOVEMBER 8

Love in Jeans smell believe turn on
     I pull them down to fuck
Then they takes them off
Put on shorts make me mad
Invents a new tennis racket

      Tennis Racket
Later someone comes by to talk
about, small straggly black hair
Love goes to hood picks up Jimmy
and drives him back buys drugs
from him →
She hides I later find but she doesn't
Know what drugs they are

THURSDAY∿∿MONDAY, NOVEMBER 12

The end of the quarter of dawn
Vigorously with mallet they make bars
he found a river and another
not wishing to wait to be lost to be
separated from the coast
to kill others, to steal, he made
the sign of the cross

Made the Christians
the islands, the infinite amount of spices
the archipelago of rivers ripe
from winter and about to flower
fifty thousand ducats

FRIDAY∿∿TUESDAY, NOVEMBER 13

Whole need stood night to
And fro progress a pass opening
to the mountains

east-south-east and west-north-west

SATURDAY∿∿WEDNESDAY, NOVEMBER 14

The wind also failed us
like the Indians
every inlet and islet full of palms
but no *mappemonde*, no clear
direction or touch of sky
into our sails   all rocky
each harbor trees perfectly still

2020 → 75th anniversary
of Holocaust closing
of Auschwitz where
will it have been then?

To go among the islands to say
marvelous things about them to find
mastic and aloe and roots to bind
from which the Indians make bread
To see fresh water we went everywhere
after a thing called desire

after 5 years in time pockets
     everything changing willy-nilly

2020 ← 75th anniversary
of Holocaust closing
of Auschwitz where
will it have been then?

I and love in future building
    she leaves me
    and I go nuts → locked up in
    escape to retrieve   ward for mental
    endure other paramours
    lies → and do but then I realize
I have fallen   <u>out of love w/HER here</u>
The Indies will do that
Film ends: (whosoever ironies here, list then)

Monday∿Friday, November 16

A thing called appetite in all places,
islands, lands to the mouth of harbors
always larger and less proportioned
than the river or creek before it peaks
into itself like a cape-height crusted
with periwinkles, pearls and a pig-like
dolphin nobody had name for all shell
and eyes we had it salted to see how

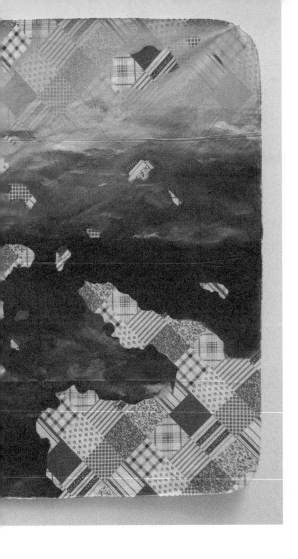

Do not fear to dream of China.
RUDOLFO ANAYA, *A Chicano in China*

After you finished your "mytho-economic epic," and for complex legal reasons, which, as always, look far simpler from a distance than when you are stuck in the middle of them, you lived in Spain for one year, hoping to clear everything up from there. A Chinese businessman and poet, whose biography of the historical Buddha you had helped to translate, helped you in turn to buy your plane ticket to Barcelona. Once there, your plan was to teach and translate English. You were fortunate to find a reliable boarding situation near the water. But there was very little work for you there, other than tending bar. So you did that, while teaching a little English, spending most of your time on a variety of translation projects. The land of the conquistadors advanced, day by day, lethargically, carrying you along in no particular direction. So you started to study Nahuatl—the language of the so-called ancient Aztecs, yet of which there are today over one million native speakers—to learn it on your own, to imagine which words in that language would have described this world, were its ancient speakers ever to have arrived on these alien shores. What would they have said and seen? What does the world look like in reverse?

In your small bedroom overlooking an alleyway that led, in two turns, to the shore, you worked at the language by translating poems into it. One of these was Ezra Pound's first canto, which begins famously on a beach scene: "And then went down to the ship,/Set keel to breakers, forth on the godly sea." Pound's poem translates a sixteenth-century Latin version of Homer's Odyssey, which took place in the Mediterranean on whose coasts you were then living, leaping in Catalan like a dolphin-crest or a monkey's momentary grammar. From there you could take a close look at the sand and salt air bunched into the forms of new gods to these shores, piled high in the agglutinative tongue of prehispanic Mexico. Here are the first lines of your translation, of which I am sure that not a single one is grammatically sound:

Auh onitemoc acallpa,
Acallaza apollonall'huic, on'amictla'teotic, auh

Ticnemitia acalquauhyollotl auh acalquachpanitl,
Tochahuan'acalco huampoh tonacauh'huan

Etia choquitzli'ca, in acalquexcochtli
Tehcatoco dir otz'tilmatli'ca, tecomahua

Circetzin, teotl inhuan otla'papua.
Niman atlan quaicalcuexcochtli

Pexoni ecatla cahu'tlayohua.
Tonatiuh cochilitzli", in the spectemur agendo

Kind of yolia came but all bounds of "Cimmerimictlan,"
And went on, "inhuan nican,"

Near precipices where lizards do push-ups, "yauitl tlillica,
Atotochmictlan, tihualtohuicaque dir amaitl

Amanalitzli Circexpan...

The gods hear you even when your grammar is bad and your words are aped. "The ocean flowing backward," reads Pound's version of these last lines, "to the place/Aforesaid by Circe." Circe is a powerful dreamer in the ancient Greek world. She comes from the lands of sorcery on the eastern shores of the Black Sea, modern-day Georgia, called then Colchis. In the ethnographic epic *Argonautica* (the story of Jason's exploits in this far east), Apollonius Rhodius describes Circe awakening from her fearsome night visions, "bathing her head in the salt sea-spray." She awakens afraid because her dreams come true: blood turned to fire, humans to animals, common herbs to witchcraft, and slime from the rainless sky. Her magic is bad translation; trickery, some said, but it is an impoverished sense of symbolic power that distinguishes between tricks, magic, miracles, and the mysterious efficaciousness of the fetish, poem, or dream. She forsakes her death so that beasts can gaze on wonders.

The magical staff she carries—like Hermes's, of whom a statue meets you when you exit the central train station of Mataró, where you lived—is forked. The Nahuatl word for forking is ohmaxac, a crossroads. Bernardino de Sahagún, the early Spanish missionary who is known as the first anthropologist of the Americas, notes in his *General History of the Things of New Spain* that the crossroad in Aztec Mexico is saturated with spiritual anxiety. There, people built roadside temples to the gods and goddesses, where small offerings could be left or, in cases of extreme ritual expiation (as when a person had badly offended the gods), it was where this unlucky soul's body was interred. These bifurcated locales were yet another instance of the interpenetrated threads that weave Mesoamerican space-time, whereupon humans can perceive the movement of the gods, or move in such a way as to disturb them (for better or worse, since some wake in sunnier moods than others, salt-air in their eye or hair). There is also the fear that some, like Circe, go around pulling too cannily on the threads, and can split and rework the strands at will into the magic of spools and coral gardens.

The backward flow splits a tide. Although you did not know it at the time, a collaborator of yours, Camille Hoffman, an artist of threads and weavings, also lived on those shores then, about two hundred miles down the coast. In 2013 you worked together on a fictional ethnography of planet Earth after climate collapse. She made the paintings and recovered ritual objects of this post-cataclysm world—such as the one above made on a plastic dime-store tablemat—and you wrote its rediscovered poetry and folklore: "Packs of creatures who could no longer remain human kept alive what ancestral rites they could remember. They listened in the forests but to nothing. And they gazed at the open sea with blank stares. The rites they could not remember they reinvented. A magus in a four-headed mask unweaves the ceremonial mat to open the gateway between this world and that. He communicates the size, material, pattern, and allowable cost of the mat to a spirit on the other end, who takes the order and sees it fulfilled. From the world of spirits the mat resurfaces. The food of their dead was melted plastic." You called this work "Partial Animals," and wrote one fragment of its folkloric "Venusian Book of Textures" to intersect with her appropriations of Theodor de Bry's sixteenth-century engraved illustrations of the cannibals of Brazil:

FROM THE *Venusian Book of Textures*

A small dacite stone fashioned into a cylindrical tool; a flake of white, translucent quartz; a bladed quartz and jarosite aggregate; a quartz crystal aggregate; several pyrite nodules that showed evidence of use; a small, worn and abraded piece of chalcedony; a magnetic andesite flake; a large chalcedony vein stone; and a small magnetic kaolinite stone naturally eroded into an unusual shape, similar to a flower but pyramidal. The last one is tracked like a reptile with deck tape for A. It is similar to a flower in that. It is a pyramid whose function is two-fold: the structure's angles and openings make a resonant chamber by which signals are received within its body which 2) is in turn used as a way to track movements of planets, stars and orbs across the sky. Its mass emits a note not unlike that which we call time. TOHR: Texture Obverse Hybrid Retrograde. It grows inside me as if there were room for another body inside my own when there is manifestly not. My shoulder is pushed into itself, a bone whose pain bears repeating, so it is pushed with nowhere to go. [...]

A serpent band of worshippers in our midst carry not light but a dark snaking shadow to the water. The water made the tempest swells, their test; they can either take dive or retreat. Who is the one who has made this their Neanderthal Tenochtitlan, endless process of making holy things? Who is the one whose shapes permeate and encompass regeneration is the one who vivifies the cosmos with newly created things. They swell inside my body where is no room inside for more. O secret of power, o fossilized word not simulated. You are touched by my predicate and a different concretion is made. They who fail to hear are by a different language made. Their language is virus although they fear infection. Their attempts to self-inoculate only made the virus stronger. Isn't this obvious that this is what should occur? Infinite values finitely determine. Apprehend and you are hence pretend a god. No predicate, no need to fear, your pretend realizes. You made the tempest, did you not? And the light that is. And the darkness too. "Who is that one who you talk to," my partner said to me, "who are you talking to?" "That man there." "What man?" The man with the gold watch.[1] [...]

Cutting my thighs through the brush, pushing the dry bushy needles and weeds apart with my arms, I made my way into the gully. The figure flashed again a few yards from me, in the denser tangle of dry reeds—a person. *Oscar?*[2] All things then were alike with no intrinsic significance

---

1 There is a tendency to life. "Is that you down there? Who are you talking to?" I hear from above. "The man with the golden watch." Who's that? "I don't know but he's there." Where? "Right there, in the corner of the room." And who are you? "I'm Oscar." What are you doing here, Oscar? "I pass through people, that's how I move." He paused again, waiting for me to go on. "It's so sad–for so many people they get here and that's it. This is the end for them. They never know how full of life the universe actually is." Have you met many other life forms? "So many. They came to me and they took me away and they told me that this planet, sick as its humans are with violence and destruction, is under quarantine. It has been purposefully isolated. None of the other people out there want anything to do with humans, not yet at least. Maybe not ever. And it's so sad because there are so many creatures out there of astonishing candor, beauty and ability."

2 "Oscar," he calls to me, but Oscar is not my name. I am a caterpillar in the time of internet and apes. My godmanship is dimmed but only because I require a continu-ing sense of self. It is glue whereas I am programmer. Aren't I? I transfer order faster than the speed of light. If it is anywhere, it is everywhere. I walk up to him, kicking dust to make my approach known. His black, shiny hair backs into the double pits of his opal eyes. He seems to me to be falling backward into his own eyes. Since he doesn't say anything, I reckon he can't speak Venusian. Why I expected this creature to speak Venusian, let alone any human language, I don't know. But I approached him that way. I mean, when I got near, an arm's length away, he looked away with the graceful movement of a reptile–his scales shiny in the quantal light. "I left you there–," I started to say, not knowing why I started my sentence that way. The enor-mous burst in my brain's size had given me remarkable abilities, but nothing that

like a new universe of distinctions and movements without difference when the dark negative spaces between the reeds pushed up more forcefully than the reeds. In this inverted tangle I saw it was not a human I had seen but a hominid with the features of an armadillo carrying the bulky form of an adult human. A fleshless skull turned on its scaly torso toward me amber eyes shifted like the moon on a river's tide. Its plated body flashed in the moon glint and was gone, like the ghost of an exterminated Neanderthal. [...]

To insist you need the word; the word itself is insistence. Insisting itself it persists. Perchance is there a vision here? I insist that there is not. "Do you get my drift?" The flaming waters hiss to the gull. Wash me in your waters when I come through the gate of invention. Beckon me with blanket and moccasin and wash me when I come stumbling underneath the light of the pilgrim moon. Measure me with your eye and wash me with your hands. Remind me to my blankness, but first make me a fire in your wet hands. The ball of light pyramidal center whereof breaks pleasure in the calm, scintillating in simple terms. Calm feels the water and the excited moss inside. Reach at my moss and take from its unrest a subtlety of excess. Each others' hands we will hand each other. An owl looks. The gulf opens exaggerated destruction, whence we stare. Upward to the creature perched issues intimations of your new birth. Heart come other way to clarity's banishment, remorseless opaque. You here consumed in the strangle of syllables, the ossified lakes of mist-girt Thoth. Or Thor? No, neither—Tohr.[3] He tore the cart toward the pageantry edge-bright crashing in. And what were his birds then? His bird was the turkey-buzzard, who also had a lesson and a song. The closely hidden song of the turkey-buzzard as she walked back to her overhang sang above his trash. He was left to himself then. And himself was left to him. But it made no difference to draw life from finite passages when his bones new bones grew inside he needed drugs. But all he had was their drugs. And their drugs gave him edge. Hard drugs. The kind you hide in your electrical outlet. Sharp as a cuttlefish he showed us he was an ape. With deck tape for A the last one crawled on its belly like a snake terrifying the ape. Why do apes, like human children, fear snakes? Primordial alterity tuft of grass shifting. Will form arise there? He will write a poem, he will. Will shape

could explain why I started my sentence that way. What I wanted to say was, "father, wherever we go we could make our songs our burdens and nobody else's. That way–" "My boy," I should have said to him, "are you all right?" "I'm all right, I think." "Your head is hot. Step out for some fresh air." I step through a noose that closes around my ankle. It lifts me like an enneagram or quadrangle of triangles. The telencephalon opens its bottom. I am hanged like the hanged man.

3 Tohr refers to the fact that you are floating with the stars, milky rivers and mills of helium. Your body is a hexakosioihexekontahexagon of light. You come through the door, drawn away from the cold by the warmth of an exquisite scene. Rest now for this too is part of the ceremony. We will sing for you in venerable majesty. Fruits and meats swell from the table whose end is touched by the sight of your eyes like lynx eyes. Chestnuts curl into a stone bowl. Herbs breathe heavily in the chest of a very large animal. The city is under his dominion. And time there slips away.

dacite chalcedony trim flake of quartz jarosite clumps inlay pyrite collect kaolinite and andesite. Confront the visible, exhaust ideas, his things. That is his god spoke. His will continue, his things. His him besides it is his habit. Come on, man. How he loves and has continuance. Come on, man, his things.[4]

---

4 We walk back across the quarry not at all wondering about those snakeheads. But, for some reason, I thought then about Tohr. His scales were like bones, his voice like a computer's. The city spread out before me like a motherboard with roads of gold night to black corporate towers of ecstasy and excess. Somewhere a celebration of passages was occurring every instant. I hardly knew I had practiced the ritual myself. He told me that I had. I went up to the dark rooms with fear dispelled from my small heart. All shapes and kinds of shifting were there, mastering one another. I lost my breath to know such eternity. Mute rock, make more of my body the sun, make it that even with the blood men splatter on your side I am permitted there like some electrical fire in the mind as massive as galaxies. Make it so that they see this and grow like you who took so long to grow. He seemed then to pause though at first I thought he was stuck for some kind of a feeling but he was waiting for me to respond. I turned out and walked through another corridor, each section of my body alighting to a blue holothermic reflection of itself. First my head, my neck and chest, then my arms and hands, then my mid torso and belly, then my hips, genitals and buttocks, and finally down into my legs and feet. I was walking now through the gully when I met a man named—I don't remember his name—but he was so parched that I had to help him, clumsily with my new body.

TUESDAY∿∿SATURDAY, NOVEMBER 17

Dreamt Talking
to M[ ]tt Sh[ ]nk
Who is dead → s[old friend]ense
didn't make sense

WEDNESDAY∿∿SUNDAY, NOVEMBER 18

Flying Rio de Janeiro
whole city → city from airport
drive thru truck

occident → woman we pick up
tells us her brother
who died falling from
suspension trolley he
had built across countries
→ US/Canada//Vancouver, Seattle

We end up at a house w/her
And she wants
But I do not want. [NAFTA?]

I become a killer somehow
Killing several people
brutally, first torturing
them then tricking them
into thinking they will
live then killing them; diary

THURSDAY∿∿MONDAY, NOVEMBER 19

Dream
Animals
Zoo

FRIDAY∿〰Tuesday, November 20

I did not wish to go to the islet
for two reasons:

the Indians taken at Guanahani
might get away

the other, because
the pizza I made was not enough
for everyone then when
fat sapiens got hungry there was
some for him → Christ-like
my reflexes stopped him
from finishing my slice

SATURDAY∿〰Wednesday, November 21

We were off the coast of Florida
Forty-two degrees but it was not hot
It was very cold, almost ice-cold

It seemed for no accident then
The wind such a sly tenant
On the permissions of the sea

SUNDAY∿〰Thursday, November 22

On Wednesday we steered south
By east, with an east wind
And it was almost calm
Into the third quarter southward
when the sun rose, we found   40 MILES
Ourselves as far from land
As the previous day
Owing to contrary currents

like a large baby's coffin
the sight of the boat in that calm light

MONDAY∿∾FRIDAY, NOVEMBER 23

Friday-People one eye in forehead
and others they call Cannibals
Who eat their words when they speak

so many living things

TUESDAY∿∾SATURDAY, NOVEMBER 24

At first we dare not approach land
we thought the sea broke heavily
at the opening to the mountain-reef
making entrance bars to lovely
river spewing out not to take us in
its palms and trees like the rest

WEDNESDAY∿∾SUNDAY, NOVEMBER 25

Noise of some stones in there
Some veins the color of gold
remembered the river Tagus
boys pleading to the pines
overstating their worth so the oaks
and strawberry trees respond
their voice the color of iron
deep and large from which a hundred
ships could be held together in fleet
        seeing the timber and pitch
clearly as tree, fruit, flower, and fungus
port and water—they drank together
and how lovely was the drunkenness
of the boys and the trees

Thursday〜〜Monday, November 26

Evening wind sank today so dark
the course of which we could never outlive
and not suffer the bliss of others
the bliss of the ones who see in this dark
these valleys accessible leafy trees
pines peopleless except for Indians
their indications their fires and signs
quadrants, customs, fears of words
swallowed by dogs who eat words

Friday〜〜Tuesday, November 27

Its peopling undulates bowl-like
shaken from below by new men
from a new world, outside
the paradigms of everyday thought

it was easy to achieve our
success because it was an accident

For this reason we must not let
any other stranger to come get
to trade or set foot here
for this is the alpha and omega
of enterprise
the arrival of one from beyond
to build town, lawn, and fort

Saturday〰Wednesday, November 28

I am in my grandmother's tiny
room in her tiny, concrete house
outside San Salvador, so close to the fields
I smell wet earth past the village trash

composite realities:
Strangely—while I am dreaming—
I also have déjà vu
and we are sitting again on her bed
where she is dead and alive too

Her bedside cabinet as usual
peopled with icons and saints
perched next to each other
sitting on top of one another
stuck with tape to the wall too
beneath other ones stuck to

Stuck to some of their bodies
are the more familiar faces of her kin:
Sister, children, ancient friends

It seems very normal to live
in collage, her scrapping-together
in the teal, tin-roofed room

Magnificent approach to mist-covered rock-falls, scarred with green sea and rosy mangrove air. Slightly seasick. I wrote a letter to myself in the future, a diary I guess, chocks of rotted fat melting in the open fire. From the rigid light of my study, I imagine it all: the problem of heroism, high tension, dejection, and all struggles for liberation from the sensual pleasure of hate. It will be complete one day, it will. Like a sobbing drunk, the anecdote will die off, you too, and all that will continue will be that idea, clear as form, reflective and electric green. No wind, no rain on and off, no superior conclusion or silvery dimness of a moonless night. But if this were to be the end—feeling that I am choking, that the claws of death are strangling me aside—and no thick soup. Oh yes—among other things I am interested in nature. My intellectual interests are alive with its color. Poisonous verdigris. Phosphorescent magenta. Saxe-blue sky-dust. I got up at 5:30 and took a walk over the shady side of the island, impression of something real. The steep side of Marx coming into my mind slow, like a deserted house from miserable trees. I checked my pockets, went back to shore and inland again. I thought about my present attitude toward ethnographic work, pessimism—ethnographic pessimism—my dislike of it, my longing for civilization. After breakfast I looked over my notes, my right leg, my stony slowness, my phlegmatic ways. Pain in my knee to overpower me. Fish leaping all around. Thoughts, feelings, moods, and my documents. I must lead an intellectual life, and live in seclusion. Coughing, thirsty. Nothing to suppress the temptation of smoking again. After breakfast, a drop of gin and ginger beer. The most important thing would be to eliminate *elements of worry out of my work*. To have a feeling of *the ultimate mastery of things*. Visions as well. The fervor of glances. The absolute value of bodies.

Sunday〰️Thursday, November 29

Like seeing a syringe at the park
Do you pick it up if so does it go
In the trash then what about the guy
Who gets the trash—if it pokes him
Or do you leave it there, not to
Make it more than another city trifle

lump of wax, where there is
lump of wax there were other good things
a man's head in a small basket
covered with another basket
hanging to a post of a house we think
must house some principal ancestors

Tuesday〰️Saturday, December 1

The room was normal me sitting
how I might in any room but something
wasn't right so I left the room
went down the hall each move
making it all more makeshift, real fake
if I push on the walls they break
running into other rooms
until I get to an open window
in a dream do you jump and if so
how do you know

Wednesday〰️Sunday, December 2

Journeys over a bridge
misplaced things // have to sob art
clearly in morning to get
right with things — jeans, shoes

THURSDAY∿∽Monday, December 3

Owing this and that, always owing
armed men came with me to ships
found creek everywhere cultivated
going along where I led them
arranged, roofed, all level
at the top there was garden we got
close to until they took out their spears
we went back through the apiary
saying by signs we should leave that
they wanted to kill us I unsheathed it
walked around that way
and came back praying that they saw it

FRIDAY∿∽Tuesday, December 4

Light wind two leagues
Along the coast past the cape
Five leagues to the next cape
And a league and a half from there
To the big river's stupid mouth

SATURDAY∿∽Wednesday, December 5

examine sunrise, the coast trended
to the south, inclined south-west
I would like to go there
but the Indians there eat their words
examine therefore harbor, Cadiz-like
carrying a light into the dark

Sunday∿Thursday, December 6

This cape is a star, that one
an elephant another a circus clown
and I have become a turtle
from one island to the next, not
doubting not having faith either
just owing everything to everyone
a kind of promontory to all life
forty fathoms deep clear, without
shoals or carracks to take apart
unsheltered except for oak
and strawberry trees medium-tall

Monday∿Friday, December 7

Bike in rain in search of my cousin's home
land in a river not very large
after midday, the lonely sunlight
like a fish asphyxiated
barely alive because of the rain
a sidewalk in Vancouver or New Orleans

Tuesday∿Saturday, December 8

Heavy rain-north wind put my hand
on the handrail purple-green beneath it
pulsing bruises on the wood

Wednesday∿∿Sunday, December

no dwelling, no death in life
no respite from the wintry month
no village at a distance
or the sea from which to come home
no contrary pace, no closure
to land, sand, or sowing
no dwelling, no superior conclusion

Thursday∿∿Monday, December 10

Some huts, some wide roads, sure,
Some places where people made fires

but nothing to stop me from taking off
my clothes to sit their mothers' mats

my bike later that day I was so worn down
I couldn't make it up the hill my

legs stuck like solid mastic
forced to walk my bike up dirt roads

FRIDAY∿∿TUESDAY, DECEMBER 11

Theatre
Vampire   Song, Seduction
Beachside eating Oysters, cop-party

Making my way w/dwarf horse
through some land of war
        → she betrays me then
        I <u>capture</u> her

That Cannibals are Grand Khan's
I have repeated

intelligent life shored up an
Earth upright a dory-like salmon
seeing itself in a sardine's eyes
teeth beneath a shrimp's beard

The theater was against one sang while
another sucked blood from behind

Majesty-like cloud-shaker
Electric-sea King
originally king of the Open

Saturday〜∿∿Wednesday, December 12

We did not set out to dream this day
for the reason that a big cross
entrance of the harbor blocked
as a sign the honor of Christendom

to see the trees and plants, the crowds
of people, all naked until we called

We were on the outside looking in
At something we could not even see

Eventually a young woman came over
lovely but lost in fear who had left
her country, her friends, everything
to dress in glass beads and brass rings

We sent her back but the sailors
who went in the boat said when they landed
that she would not leave the boat
that she wanted to stay with other Indian
women we had taken at Juana Banana

Other Indians appeared at the entrance
of the harbor and saw the ships, the cross
and turned back

so she showed them the village situation
which is when they saw
the small piece of gold
in her nose another indication

Sunday∿∿Thursday, December 13

The three men gone
with the woman came back shitless

It was the middle of the night
and they stayed up until dawn
telling us that they had seen

a wall scrawled with crosses
and names of people who
died trying to cross

to the other side
inhabitants crammed the valley
chewing roots as mainstay

people of character hungry
even beautiful ones, white
as any you could find in Spain

perhaps even more white
than the green plains of Cordoba
full of fruit and breezes and

nightingales singing red
crickets, frogs and cotton trees
the wall kept them from so

tired even time was slower
there sand moved almost in error

MONDAY∿∾FRIDAY, DECEMBER 14

turtle at the end of the world
one arm in the sea and the other
pulling against the current
of a river coming down
mountain and valley to beach

TUESDAY∿∾SATURDAY, DECEMBER 15

To examine, to reach, to enter,
to voyage, to wish, to occasion,
to send, to fathom, to flow openly,
to be in the middle of a valley
to hunt, to point, to look
and leave behind, to give something
a name, a case, a type of signal—
are all the same kind of inaccessible.

Wednesday〜〜Sunday, December 16th

At midnight I left my body
with a light land breeze going
from the gulf following
a colorful field into streets
up scaffolds into buildings and back
down into my mental powers
like a sandal mid-channel waiting
for my foot

Then one by one came many at once
wearing nothing and wanting nothing
except to share names
saying one another's names secretly
in their group in nice voices

in gardens pregnant with desire
in mouthfuls of bread and water

In a desert maybe? Something.
Something to do with that and lizards,
Big ones. But not dinosaurs.

Thursday〜〜Monday, December 17

More scaffolding for a building
came out of my bed with nets
and sharp, large sticks hardened
in a fire and placed in my hand
like a stone I throw into the water
to settle the disembarked people
of my dreams, of the drag-canoe

Friday∿Tuesday, December 18

With more than two hundred men
the King took us to his house
to seat us at his table

The Queen apparently was gone
and we made a mess of everything

Others started to clean up
we put the place together, sort of
because I was busy discovering
their things, their thin treasures

He put me on a bus back to town
but the driver of the bus
did not want to end the party
did not want to stop the carnival

So she made the passengers dance
everyone acting sexual
completely shouldered by the wonder
of their singing thick pleasures

I showed my genitals to a man
behind me and to his right a woman
who told me I must be dreaming
or in a false awakening
because this is not usually what I do

It's true I don't but by that time
we were already in full intercourse

Saturday〰Wednesday, December 19

Someone writes their dissertation
about this night, fourteen hours long
during which I realize, at the bay's end
where the river bends off,
that I am the island distance staring

down at myself, damned
to abstraction because of what I did.

Later on, I'm sitting in their job-talk
with its requisite sections like

grass islands at the mall leading
no place pretending I don't know

or that I wasn't also there, zoned

Sunday〰Thursday, December 20

Picture a scorpion on your chest
stopping at its mid-gap to hoist
& pierce its stinger in your heart
Can you see that? Then picture
the same but without your skin

the stinger puncture straight
into the rose-blue beating heart

That's what happened to the reefs

not once, but over and over
until it got thick with poison-air

It happened inside my bed-tuck
slipped like air between sheets
of spider-webs you can shake
to scamper the spiders but can't
wake while they're crawling all
in there on you the scorpions in
way of passage   ❑◆♏❑
in a carbon-foisted interference

> *Between "there came to me in a dream" and*
> *"I dreamt" lie the ages of the world.*
> THEODOR ADORNO, *Minima Moralia*

Every decade or so, my father disappears. This time it is to Mexico City; the time before, to Maryland; before that, Guatemala; and before that, San Francisco. I hear he might be on his way to Cuba, by way of Guatemala. It looks as if he will stay there. But in a few months, when he returns, his manner is so unburdened, so devoid of worry or blame, you'd think nothing had happened. From one trip he came back with a shoebox of sculptures in clay and igneous rock. So his cousin told him, he had found these at an industrial dig in the northeast highlands of the country of Guatemala. One of them looks down from a nearby bookshelf, a seated figure holding a bowl whose sculpted handicraft mirrors that of the seated figure. Both are placed thus into the abyss, as the art term puts it, a mise en abyme that reproduces without end the image in perfect, integral form. Here, though, reproduction is interrupted, since it is not the case that the seated figure holds another seated figure. It is only by a conceptual resemblance between clay bowl-maker and bowl that the scene can be said to be abysmal.

In his "Frazerian-style" around-the-world study of kinship, anthropologist Marshall Sahlins describes cultures that distinguish parental activity from a poetics of substance. Such activity typically depends on some metaphor of substance to stay motivated: blood, element, loyalty, pride, race, fear, history, flow, land, clay. But the fact is that these substances are principally metaphors, arbitrary and unconscious, through which the experience of self and relation is organized. The study of such poetic relations interrupts the metaphor's sleeping, makes it speak for itself as a metaphor. The bowl-maker suddenly looks cautiously at the clay bowls: what is the design through which these things have come to me? What myth, narrative, ideology, lexicon, or poetry? What style of vessel, shoebox or fired Earth?

The Story of the Bowl

Holy begetting, winged serpent! A rough cereal was served and many did not come to the table. We feared again that they would sink into sameness; at this, there were tumults all over. A window here was shattered. Do I need to tell you the rest? At the same time that I was still trying to grab hold of beautiful things, I knew that you had learned of what had happened here and would be expecting an explanation from me. So it is that I sat down this morning to write these words to you:

> Tell me the word with which
> to begin a poem and with that
> will I like a locust
> accord into the wood, be not
> driven off or shot
> like an arrow to the ends of the earth
> but quake
> from the deep as does a wave
> whose fish is disturbed
> and flaps off over field after field
> thus will I sit in a hollow
> a vineyard ungathered
> and occupy there the elbow
> of a branch or thought
> that was had but not said
> a squirrel dead in the trunk of a tree
> a sandal dropped in the meadow
> between the reeds
> a reed
> stuck in the clothes of the four-

cornered mountain
entranceway to roads in the sky
entranceway to roads on the earth
    so it is that such
things are lost that way, where

I stopped writing here to observe a group of goats galloping with
the great force of mountains, a diamond that pours into a gnarly
wooden cup, a rosy thorn that cuts the anemone, and the arcane
perfections that enter the eye. I'm not easily swindled. I have seen
the birth of watery stars that left the borders of the cosmos aflame.
There I met the turtle, swelling with blood, who tossed his ass
through a flaming bush and threw his head back through death in
generation and generation in death. The sun's horrible cry shatters
the peace of the heavenly abode, he said, formulaically. A Qliphoth
or husk of corn walking the fleshless fields flips through a tattered
notebook. Another page flips. I returned to continue to write these
words to you:

When it is no longer incarnated
no longer red from green or

Incorporated or culled from like myth
of direct form of intuition
of seeming self-evidence animated
suspended between it
and some thing
pressing down into it your spirit
when it is no longer supremely forceful
arriving like order to primary forces
when the moon is unrolled
over the sea and the sea surges
at itself like wild buckwheat
that no longer shines like the fox fur
and the fox no longer sleeps with its fur
in the gully or hunts
the flow of midnight bathes
every silent throne and countless thorns
pierce the noon of high America

And some saw the destroyers
like a lightning flash of voices and heavy hail
and said these destroyers

of the earth by the earth will be destroyed
both small and great
generally and in particulars
the time will come when the rage
of nations will know greater wrath
than that of woeful reign

When it is no longer incarnated
no longer red from the beloved shoot

I am the serpent who tastes its own eye, my fire stares out from
destruction. I awaken to it, like man to his loneliness, stretching
over counters and across streets. I walk as if with feet into its sun
and wind destroying me. I disparage the sunlight. Step on my own
back and push my face into the dirt. I try again to rise up, like a
tree to bifurcations, splitting to prayer and silence. Whispering.
And then I step off, a star falling to earth, a meteor headed through
the mesosphere to collision with my crawling shape. My body is
fish through open air. I am silenced by my upper neck. There is
some kind of swimming there. I follow deeper into the water, where
I dream that I am a fat turtle swinging my ass through piles of
leaves. I laugh, sticking my head into a shell while a boy walks by
not noticing me. I am an old fart with wrinkles all over and weird
ideas about economics. I think that people are searching through
my trash, so I throw fewer things away. I remember many things
that have happened to me. Sometimes I experience déjà vu thirty
or forty times a day. When I crawl off to calm myself I stop again
thinking I've already tried crawling this way and without avail. My
tongue presses frustrated worms against the roof of my mouth but
I prefer the water. My body is fish with hardened scales. Inside its
liver regenerate the folds to be used for prophecy. I read the folds
on the tissue of blood and write the meaning out on the sand. Hom-
inids squat to see my translation but they do not understand. They
watch me go back and forth on a platform. That beast, they whis-
per to themselves. I am beast with hot breath in the cool dawn. My
power animal is the gnat. The land flows out from his eye in deltas
of piercing angle. His wings cut across the wind like scissors, erratic
and glittering. They fly up from the grass and circle above me,
looking down, shining eyes fearless and dull, a faint blur through
the clear sky. I follow him and share his fearlessness and exaltation.
When the molt thickens around my eye, I lose him. I wait, dimmed
by the fading light until I find him again twisting like a raised blade
of grass in the luminous air. He grows out of it like a cloud. It is

cool like the dawn, if it can be that the dawn is seen inclined verti-
cally like a pool. I bend my head into the pool, entering the hollow
but stop halfway. Half of me inside with the other out, half a clock
of blood thuds in time cradled beside a silent twin. There is no
speaking to him then, powerful and without form. Mist from silence
issues effect moving without words; it collects dissipated moisture to
a throne. Pulling back I am taken with a thought onto the throne,
cool on my ass. And I hear him like a creature walking around on
the roof above me. The room is palatial and although I am in it, I
am not of it. Like a cock from its coop my boned feet to exposure
step where I follow. I am thrilled by the howl of coyotes, although I
fear them more than anything else. Those who walk silently in the
shimmer of the moon force my ear wide open to the subtlest pieces
of sound, the breath of trees and the hissing of shadows all over
the hills swallowed whole by my mind. I am voracious for tones,
parallels and perpendiculars. My claws leave definite lines measur-
ing infinitude in miniature perceptions. I get ecstatic in attention,
in spite of myself. I am winged. I see it in the mirror, still every time
it shocks me. I coil my wings into shells, a form of fire. If I had a
hood, I'd hear a roar of lions when I pulled it back from my neck.

the story of the fish who ate
the sea or the rabbit
who swallowed the limbless fish
the tide is itself
its opposite and forcible bend
the people pushing toward refutation
meager push
while the eel dreams of limbs

Taken into a bathhouse wow
where I saw in their bodies
the bodies of people I have known
so liberal so familiar so plain

so one woman came to kiss me
and cuddled me and petted me like
I was a little parrot and wow
I was fine with that worked up
and wound into her arms like
a cotton ball or a patch of lace

When she left I saw an old friend
Carlos pulling a lizard off the wall
and about to pull its legs off
but I stopped him and said
what're you going to do that for?
And I took the lizard from him
And tossed it out into a bush

Later that day I came to a bad marsh
Drugs, prostitution, all that
and tried talking to them about it
with reason first then with magical
spells but they didn't care
they threatened and tried to intimidate

I left and came back with a gun
and found one of them, one of the gang-leaders,
in an abandoned lot behind a truck
fucking someone

I cocked my gun said goodbye
and shot a few times into his chest
before the gruesome last shot
into his head

Wednesday∿∿Sunday, December 23

Lord of the ship with news
Of nothing and no new change
Very cheaply, very whatever
These were his words
the words of the Indian who took two
into his village on the canoe
rowing fast about three leagues
SE of the promontory

Up to that time we had not
been able to say whether by cacique
they meant King or Governor

Up to that time we had not
been able to know that nitanyo
meant grandee

Up to that time we could not tell
if by nitanyo they meant hidalgo,
governor, or judge

The cacique met the two
in the village of two thousand
with cotton cloths, parrots,
and pieces of gold
Lords of the ships with no relic
Of evening and the wish to depart
Wait until the next day
Very patiently, very okay
Carrying the things we give you

Back to your boats to your
Place outside the river

I came upon him in the late night
lying at the edge of his bed
myself in the guise of a lion
who turned as I heard his groan so painful
inside me I fled
as he woke up, erect, ready for sex

Friday∿∿Tuesday, December 25

I got picked up in a car, I guess,
my bike was in it next to me back
in school a boy was left
to steer the ship, a thing that had
always been forbidden on the trip

whether there was wind or calm nobody
was to leave the steering to the boys

But it was Christmas, we had just met
the King, and everyone was drunk
so they sent me to do it
in the sea like in a bowl, dead calm
and everyone down to sleep

so knocked out nobody noticed
when the current carried the ship
onto one of the banks so gently
only my scream at the sound
of the breaking sea woke them, screaming

then at me, each other, some running
away in a smaller car when the ship
tilted to its side in the shallow still

close to dawn its seams opened
and the Indian canoes came to unload it
so great the diligence and haste
of the King who kept watch
over the stuff so nobody would steal it

not even the loss of a boy's shoestring

The King's Indians felt so bad about it
they brought us all kinds of gold pieces
some as big as a man's hand
and shaped like a long shrimp

In return we gave them weapons—
Turkish bows, arrows, shirts,
and gloves for their war with the Khan
and his cannibal army
Our Lord Christ making it clear
with the catastrophe what he wants

to build fort, order tower, arm
the skill of these people with weaponry

I praised the boy for his stupidity
which found in its way
the service of Christ our Anchor
of gold in these islands

He came back to say the island
larger than Portugal with twice
the people had things all over
not locked up he came back
on a new bike—a BMX he said
        in   → like in LA
             or the IE ↙
       inland Empire
he hesitated at first to take it but
the way he grew up
        you don't hesitate
        with stuff left unlocked

"When you are thirty years old
Everyone calls you young..." begins
my favorite poem, a poem
by Paul Celan, which talks about a King
who gives all his gold to a young
soldier from a distant land
because he wants him to stay with him

But the soldier, who doesn't feel so young
forcibly leaves which forces the King
to abandon his gold—his gold pieces,
gold clothing, gold canoes—
to follow him

Far away from home
memories crowd him like they did
last night in my cabin in my bed:

Dreamt at last about
        A Christian Woman →
woman I had known before
but older now still stiff and bark-like
like a birch white tree took me
into her branches, chlorophyllic
same thrill then before coitus
saw people outside the window
in the bushes looking in I stopped

a disturbance with the attractions
some had to be cut off
but in the craziness of things
I saw visitors, circuits; uses of circuits

Monday∿Friday, December 28

I ask my tío where they are from
before Guatemala City
Xela, Huehuetenango he says
       over a map, Mayan capitals
near Chiapas, K'iche' and Mam

which is not a dream with everyone
around me
       building in the day
and eating and drinking at night

our conversation as usual ends
on the topic of UFOs
my tío has seen
here, in Arizona, and Guatemala

high neon velocity in the sky
I stare into the mouth
of one the Indians whose lip
is pierced so he puts in a
neon hoop when he speaks it
       lights up bright green

Wednesday∿Sunday, December 30

I went ashore to eat, the park
by the water was very nice, where
a guy—me, really—had been shot
through his left-stomach and head

But alive like that with huge
holes in his body, like a raccoon's
last moments we saw right through
said that's what he wanted for us

his way of breaking the rhubarb
from the root, the pear from all the talk
of empire, dominion, and ploy
to keep out us immigrants—he said it

like that—we must seek tolerance
and measures of equality in all things
so the greatest things strengthen us—
he said—and the weakest not enfeeble

Toward the end of the day's work, hidden longings come to the surface, and boats as well. At moments I longed violently to go *South* again. It occurred to me that the purpose in keeping a diary and trying to control one's life and thoughts at every moment must be to consolidate life, to integrate one's thinking, to avoid fragmenting themes—marvelous reflection making fishes light up. Brutishly sensual. Animal-like. A motion of waves oozes through the clammy air: to feel it beating inside you as you type, evening, at moments sad. But not stifling. Nerves, heart. (Have I smoked too much?) After writing diary went to bathe in sea to feel it in my bones; inability to concentrate. When I was a boy I felt it was impossible. Terrible reports. I lay on my bed as if dead, asking Christ to save me from school. New idea: I am happy that I don't have to think about it very much. I feel none of the metaphysical sadness of white writers in the tropics. Dogs howling, wind in the rippled anchorage. The noise of foaming eddies. The smells of seaweed salted with indolence. I left school at the right time, expelled rather. Vegetation nestling in gaps, clusters there, tuberoses I think. I felt "innervated."

For all that, I decide to resist and work—business as usual, despite everything. Went continually back to schooldays. Racial tension like a pressure in the eyeballs, being crushed by things you have to overcome. Break in work. Turned in at 10:30.

THURSDAY∿∿MONDAY, DECEMBER 31

World apocalypse few survive
I am caved in by ideas of nature

Ides when everyone died... so many
That those who survived
Couldn't tell if anyone else was alive

☀ ☀ ☀ ☀ ☀

It's dangerous to go to the underworld
but that's what we did for them
bad seeds from a bad stock   planted
to get them out of it and because
they wanted to die

I wondered what the therapy programs
would be like for them in hell
where we went
nice houses everything so familiar
I forgot I wanted to sprout back

me and a woman I loved or was she
also part of the digger-skin paranoia

☀ ☀ ☀ ☀ ☀

so few survived she not make it
except as a ghost spading the camp

Friday∿Tuesday, January 1

Another dream of earthquake
Big one in California

Taking down buildings
Sideways, killing many

Coyote-Wife's house
Undamaged, love there ok

Is this a prediction?
Is this the fate of what left

Insinuated in its analyses
Makes caca from cacao and
                    cacahuates

Saturday∿Wednesday, January 2

One nitanyo keeps a cougar-pet
inside its cactus-mouth daggered
red and yellow who knows
what tensely has slipped in there?

One boy in particular is sent
to feed it he goes naked—no
surprise, right?—he shows off
his sham fight and what taunts

he's taught it mean "don't kill"
but how can he control that?

Watching them wrestle I forgot
they were naked his muscles
intertwined to cougar's so he
went with into its lurking and left

wearing its skin, a champion

They—*they* means the people
peptide contours—they treat me
like a cup, a protein, some *thing*
without memory, maybe feeling
but fundamentally dumb, demented
to tell me that he is lost, misplaced
like some other *thing*
when I know that he is broken,
a betrayer, Martin Alonzo, my friend

Even through my dementia
I can see it like a landscape, a sight
and raindrop to my eye while I yawn
apart, not inside, not knowing it

that he is broken like a cup, a protein
some *thing* that sailed off which
I saw but could not control, a sight

They means also those in control

Monday∿ᘖFriday, January 4

Of the twelve labors the Great Khan
Stronghold of Tiryns ✌ tasked to me
the first was to tame   ∿ ∿ ∿
            → Twelve Rivers
            → the Impossible Princess
to court and seduce him for the Khan
which I did ✌ under the nose of the Rivers's
                    LOVER
And slipped the message to the Khan
∿ ∿ ∿   just as the ship's dogs
woke me with their
barking monkeying howls and yawns

TUESDAY∿∾SATURDAY, JANUARY 5

Labors two and three were to fight
Iron Mike Tyson then to fly
out of that small island, whose face
fights had sanded to perpetual low tide
       shallow stretch, liquid tarmac
dragged doubt into my fire, could I
Punch out Iron Mike?

Grizzled Angel, the Sacred Turkey

I am in a conference room debriefing
my silver victory, my flight to Mars
       with old friends there
         appearing green
at the red mountains stream-like
chaining up to my ship

a twisted line of live beds
covers the rust of land, so high, so very
large going under the fighting heat

WEDNESDAY∿∾SUNDAY, JANUARY 6

my skull is a sea cow for this one

Dream that I write this poem
but it is not like this   Making
ghost art with glue
        & colorful bits

                    kelp
                on our faces
laced   w/feces
from the agar & mastic trees

resins of balsamic musk
to bead away the ocean water

where you'd find a flight of stairs
where LOVE finally   But
my hands caught
        w/what I'm doing

                I can't
                pay attention

FRIDAY~∿~TUESDAY, JANUARY 8

Is this Cibola, the 7th labor?

They were in Zuni Pueblo
Looking over icons
Don't kid yourself
Someone says to him
Thinking that you can control those things
    Cartoonish dangerous
Figures w white dog faces
Like Peg-Leg Pete a living index

Old friend tells him to loosen up
He hates that for reasons he has
To say because he used
To be loose, laid back outgoing

But then things people said about him
were so racist
Not serious, lazy, creative but unfocused
   These are real things
But it was also Connecticut, Colón
Combed through, that time
Tells him why he is not so loose

White spandex of a kind primarily
White dog faces playing devil on him

Headland a long plain
crosswind-fed reefs
tortoise wood shields
sirens not so beautiful
not delaying not good
but fast evil manateeish

made up my mind
about Martin Alonzo
who was my friend
appearance, a game
the name of our Lord
meant nothing we
found that for which
we came—and now
will go back—now
before evil outsteps us

pulls us into its plain

I am wasting time, while it is my duty to work as hard as possible and achieve a "position" in relation to myself—to be someone who really accomplished something; *make my mark in the world*. I must master the *mental froth* that accompanies all ambitious plans and thoughts. The eyes turn to form, its surface like a memory emerging from white amnesiac foam. The cold crystals of the foam burst in the effort. I look over my notes and add to them. Cold, overcast day. The feeling of being at the "bottom of consciousness"—"ethnographic surrealism," dependence on the dreamtime—the feeling that every thought that flows in some psychic plasma has been formed inside the organism. Inner economy. Drizzling, the damp road. Flashes of understanding, cobalt intimations, and visions of the past, like tiny copper details, continual memories and associations, ochre feelings. Thoughts: a "diary" is a history that proposes a theoretical view of self. Experience in writing leads to profound contradiction. Consequently, we cannot speak of objectively existing selves: diary creates self. Consequently, self is consciousness of contradiction. Is observation of events in keeping with a certain theory; an application of this theory to the events as personal time gives birth to the diary. Moral: most important of all is to eliminate desires for transcendence, metaphysical longings, when inner resources are insufficient. The frogs and purple sunsets there are no less scorched by the glow of history and the sapphire water of other creatures. Half-burned bits of poetry float in the air. We walked along that cliff to the beach, its golden tones complicated by other misty people. Exactly like a Turkish bath. I stopped because of my eyes, which had hardened into hot stones. Then I felt a certain relief: began to look at all this— through all this—from outside. These are Malinowksi's words. Painful feeling that he had spoiled it all in those diaries, and had, feeling for points of contact with absent ones and instances of repulsion for those present, this fundamental error and wreck to cast a shadow over personal life, over a particular personality. Flowing backward like vomit.

SUNDAY∿∿THURSDAY, JANUARY 10

Full of sand we pose take pics
in a cave of humans before the desert
discussing heroes, exploits

Regis Debray and so on

wondering why he lived; he lived
because of letters from de Gaulle,
Sartre, Malraux

I am dining w/these men trying
                    to discuss it
but I'm not to join the conversation
this is their talk about them

their cave of humans—their crystal
wall, their potash and lead

MONDAY∿∿FRIDAY, JANUARY 11

in church during a sermon
someone stands up some message
that is all benefit from the death
            trust fund of 1492/93
set up here on this beach
from east to west eighteen leagues

to go east now with the news
the DEVIL we did not evade
did not kill but coaxed instead
into the mask of maize-husks
            to make him dance it

to blind and to pummel skull
but not kill the hoodwinked DEVIL
lively, lithe, in green reeds good

he poked toward us from the marsh
tilted such sideways as arctic sun
in purple sky like what kind
of planet is this? what pictographic thrum

of prisoners without words to write?
without earth to turn to?
            sand melting like ice

TUESDAY⌇SATURDAY, JANUARY 12

Delfin, my father's friend, around
Echo Park was it driving around
→ with him in the blame
of cigarette smoke that killed him
wondering about his chicken gods
Santero from Cuba summer
in December warming Earth to talk
to the warehouse-men of dreams
popcorn gods giving out samples
turns up he says all of rock
in your mouth so you have speech
but all fled for water who left
I learned because Castro locked up
in prison years and then sent him
to Madrid then somehow LA

Anamnesic mermaid fin glimpses

Dooku who is my friend
Can you believe that
Cristobal and Ct. Dooku
He who holds Christ in his heart
and Pinzón of the planet Serreno
            making friends
Until my emperor's command
That I kill him and inside me
Any affection I had
his head rested facedown on the rock
my sword-face met without falter

the planet exploded with that strike
like today when the Indians,
like Cannibals
finally turned tooth on us

I was in bed with a boy, myself?,
Or was it a girl, I can't remember
promising to spend next Christmas
together in bed, eating takeout
Chinese if we had to
when I heard the news that
our Christian soldiers had been
tricked and turned upon on
the beach, on the fuzzy TV
bows shooting arrows at them rocks
also lobbed, dogs shouting pigs
firing shit-wild in the sand white
Christians drew their sword-faces
& the lizard people backed off

we could tell the planet was done
for, tho, exploded in that scene

THURSDAY∿ϾMONDAY, JANUARY 14

It was his brothers, magicians
high sea running not
the Man himself that brought
him back to life   a sign

The resurrected King

a biscuit in honey whose bright
awakened eye so real
so lifelike with red cap
beads, red cloth, & gold mask

we thought we were ready, caulked

and to sail but something wasn't
right w/the work, much water
leak at the keel and the bed
damp with morning light but
                           the carriage
dark as midnight pitch sticks
floating in promise of our King

Will this be the one labor?

His brothers brought a woman
back a witch they said who had
looks of time sped x3
our hours titrate just to stare at her

So I said we would go on like that
with her, trusting in our Lord
to lead us back
those were my words

Friday〜〜Tuesday, January 15

Dinner gone awry
I drag myself home
Thru new zones
New areas in my town
I had never noticed
Crawling my way
Thru and then out
With a boy I take
To the movies drinks
Late he is eight
And I out w Drunk
Discussing horrifying
Notion that he has
Just purchased a car
To speed us home

NOTES

Colonoscopy

1: With an eye to Odysseus, this book begins in a cave of etymons and puns. The etymological wordplay is of a kind with Odysseus's escape from the cave of the Cyclops Polyphemus by way of a linguistic ruse. Odysseus's ruse is to tell the Cyclops that his name is "*Udeis*," which means "nobody," so when the drunken Cyclops—blinded by Odysseus driving a stake in his eye—cries out to his Cyclopean kin, he is left unassisted because "nobody" has hurt him. In *Dialectic of Enlightenment*—the classic study of how "myth is already enlightenment, and enlightenment reverts to mythology"—Max Horkheimer and Theodor Adorno describe Odysseus's ruse as a magical act that undoes the spell of origins. In their account, *origin* is the complete unchangeable fusion of word with thing ("nobody" fused with the body trapped in the cave) that is the primordial Cyclops's way of seeing things. Odysseus's cunning is to "exploit the difference." His poetic fraudulence exploits the contingency of names, and therefore lets him and his crew sneak to freedom. But therein is the colonial stain. Horkheimer and Adorno point out that Odysseus has to "disown himself as Nobody" to "declare allegiance to himself." In denying his own identity, preserving his life by way of a fraudulent legalism, he preserves the language of his capturer, effectively fleeing with that capturer's systems of power and law entwined in his body. If he has so deeply identified with his oppressor can he be said, then, to be free? How is it possible to flee when every vocal step will be stained with that originary mimesis, a model of its own domination? Horkheimer and Adorno's answer here is that the duplicity or doubling undoes the singular totality of the Cyclops' world. Unlike the blinded giant, Odysseus leaves the cave conscious of the mediation and its contradiction—capable of a kind of intentionality in contradiction called "critical theory." Actually, he is not entirely there yet. When he leaves the cave, he shouts from a distance his real name to distinguish his identity from nothingness (but also, Horkheimer and Adorno suggest, to proclaim the "fragile advantage the word has over violence"). From this act unfolds the entire epic. Polyphemus reports this bandit by name to his father, Poseidon, who curses the hero to wander the seas. This anxious compulsion to cling to the power of his name perpetuates "the calamity which enlightened language brings on itself." It is at that moment that myth and enlightenment are revealed to be crossed strands in a tense weaving—a crisis of "mythistory," as described in the notes below. As Tiresias prophesies, it is not until Odysseus learns to value catachresis—to value the mistaking of an oar for a winnowing fan, that is, to value the temporal disalignment and contradiction created by the abuses of signs and their objects—that the hero's curse is lifted.

3: I made this collage in spring 2015, combining elements from Quechua chronicler Felipe Guaman Poma de Ayala's *Primer Nueva Corónica y Buen Govierno*, Gustave Doré's illustrations for Dante's *Divina Commedia*, and William Blake's illustrations for the *Book of Job*. Guaman Poma de Ayala's chronicle (written in the early 1600s) is a Quechua account of the conquest-wars of the Andes, describing the conflicts between native and non-native cultures, and the obnoxious behavior of the Spaniards. Written for King Philip III of Spain, it explained to the Spanish king that governance without meaningful integration of native societies was not possible, fostering only conflict and violence. But the work was lost in its journey across the Atlantic, not reemerging until the German Egyptologist Richard Pietschmann found it in the Royal Danish Library in Copenhagen in 1908. The image incorporated in the collage depicts the story of a captain named Cuci Uanan Chire Ynga, who sips first from the power of his father, the sun, before going into battle. The bodies headfirst in the pits that Dante and Virgil examine—and which Dante bends over to whiff—are the simoniacs of the eighth circle of hell. Here, in the third bolgia of the circle, are punished those who sell pardons; it is a moment when Dante condemns the various popes of the early fourteenth century to hell for complex fraud. Blake painted Satan smiting Job with sores around 1826, after he finished the last and longest of his prophetic books, *Jerusalem: The Emanation of the Giant Albion*. In this work, as in all of Blake's writings, Satan is a rebel and hero, a troublesome spiritual liberator akin to Christ. The image that I used in the collage does not satisfactorily convey the tempera painting from which it is sourced, in which Satan's dark skin and sideways-twisted body are reminiscent of Blake's 1796 illustration of "A Negro Hung Alive by the Ribs" for the soldier-historian John Gabriel Stedman's account of the Dutch colony at Surinam. Dutch masters there made cock-a-hoops of the art of colonial mastery. As in the 1796 illustration, Blake's 1826 Satan hangs over a coastline, recirculating the fires of a wagered rebellion. In the interaction of these various chronologies of conflict, condemnation, rebellion, war, resistance, and redemption, the collage returns to the spirit of Guaman Poma de Ayala's letter to the Spanish king. Recent political theory of the Andes has confirmed that the only viable jurisgenerative model for the region is plurinational statehood. The concept—ratified in the 2009 constitution of the newly named Plurinational State of Bolivia—emerged as a means of organizing the autonomy of the various indigenous and non-indigenous societies, polities, and cultures that co-exist in Bolivia. As Bolivian intellectuals René Zavaleta Mercado, Luis Tapia, and Javier Sanjinés have argued, at issue in the concept of plurinational statehood is a departure from the violence of a unidirectional historicism inescapably culminating in western modernity and neoliberalism. Rather than assume that economic liberalization is the ineluctable end of temporal progress, Bolivian plurinationalism aspires to reckon with the other conceptions of the world by which people shape their experiences of time. This involves the indigenous cultures of the Andes, as well as the temporal heterogeneity of mestizo itinerants and other immigrants. Sanjines makes the compelling argument that the US and Europe could learn from this model, in as much as current migration crises there are deepening the rifts between states and their national identifications, eroding the self-surety of indivisible, unchanging, singular nationalism. A singular nationalism will only perpetuate investments in a never-realizable singular modernity, whose unrealizability is marked by the violence of borders and immigration fascism, the cruel dream of national purification programs. An aesthetic form invested with such temporal heterogeneity—whose underlying political theory is that of the totalizable fragment—is the collage.

University Head

11 Out of discretion and concern for privacy, I use family and friends' names in this book minimally.

12 The Universidad de San Carlos emerged from the Colegio de Santo Tomás Aquino—founded in the city of Santiago de los Caballeros in 1562—that was destroyed by earthquakes in 1773.

The Guatemalan Civil War, one of the most brutal conflicts in Latin America between a US-backed military junta and leftist rebel groups backed by indigenous and mestizo peasants, lasted from November 1960 to December 1996.

Gregorio Yujá Xoná was killed in one of the many shocking incidents of the war. After having exhausted all avenues to publish their protests, a group of K'iche' peasants ambushed the Spanish Embassy to bring greater attention to their cause. The Guatemalan police reacted harshly, firebombing the embassy to clear out the protesters. Only Yujá Xoná and the Spanish ambassador, Máximo Cajal López, survived. Both were taken to the hospital, whence the ambassador was snuck out of the country by the Costa Rican ambassador, while Yujá Xoná was kidnapped by the counter-revolutionary lynch mob. His body is buried in the central campus of the University.

Our first cousin once removed is Luis Augusto Turcios Lima, who died in 1966 (25 years old) in a roadside explosion while fighting for FAR. I am told that there is a statue of him and a school in his name in Cuba. He is somewhat of a mythic figure in our family history. At 15 he enlisted in the Guatemalan army, from which he was sent to train at the infamous US Army School of the Americas in Fort Benning, Georgia—essentially a finishing school for anti-communist dictators and death-squadron leaders in the southern cone, noting among its alumni Roberto D'Aubuisson, Efraín Ríos Montt, Manuel Contreras, Guillermo Rodríguez, and Manuel Noriega. After his return, Turcios Lima turned sides to fight on behalf of the guerrillas. Eduardo Galeano wrote about him in his *Guatemala: Occupied Country* (1968): "The previous leader of the Rebel Armed Forces, Luis Augusto Turcios, was also a legendary figure for the peasants, who attributed supernatural virtues to him. He was a hot-blooded young officer who learned the technique of the guerrilla from the Yanquis themselves—in a course at Fort Benning, Columbus, GA, on how to combat it. Dictator Peralta Azurdia put a price on his head and he put one on dictator Peralta Azurdia's. After he took to the hills in 1960, he mocked death a thousand times. Absurdly, death won because his car caught fire on the highway." From his own writings, it can be seen that Turcios Lima (like many of his generation) was influenced by the ideas of the Peruvian philosopher José Carlos Mariátegui. Mariátegui argued that a class-based analysis of the peasants of Latin America was impossible without reckoning with colonial racialization, because modernization in the

Americas was nourished by the racial subjugation of black and indigenous people (1928). Mariátegui's works drew not just from Marx, but also from the knowledge, experiences, and patterns of life indigenous to the Americas. On this note, César Montes's biography of Turcios Lima, published in Havana in 1968 (which I lineated at one point for another epic—in collage form), reads:

Sabemos ahora—o no?—que los cantos
Luctuosos deben entonarse con canto
De ametralladora. Frente Edgar Ibarra un
proceso revolucionario desenvolviéndose
rompiendo con los esquemas y dogmas
del marxismo Viejo, en un alto ritmo
"no temo muerte," Turcios en ritmo, "la
revolución guatemalteca seguirá su curso"
un caso teniendo nada de excepcional
muriendo sin saber lo que representaba

para movimentos guerrilleros latinoamericanos
y del mundo; delgado, desgarbado, de ojos
verdes como la serpiente que mira
en silencio pero sin perder ningún movimiento
sentado en suelo y enlodado
"caramba," dijo un campesino, "es más
grande el nombre que su dueño..."

Another way of thinking about the classic Marxist concept of subsumption is in terms of rhythm; what are the rhythms that organize your social and political life; what are the syncopations or arrhythmias by which seeming wholes are revealed to be so many discrepant parts, holding together as a configuration, yet one in which each part is able to subsume you into its full experience (i.e. the totalizable fragment). The point is not that one temporal scheme resolves another; rather, the point is that the conflict between temporal schemes proves the contingency and possibility of social life. Time is not captive to late capitalism (or the Hegelian historicism from which that concept derives). Time is unequal and contested, an interaction of parts in constant catachresis. The catachresis stages the temporal inconstancies through which flow all sorts of political agency. I was inspired to work on this poem-collage when—in graduate school—I discovered a trove of documents related to my first cousin once removed. Initially, I thought it was strange to come across his documentation in Yale's Beinecke Rare Book and Manuscript Library. But, when I learned that the library's foundation had been interwoven with the OSS and CIA, particularly through the efforts of Norman Holmes Pearson and James Jesus Angleton, it was obvious why documents pertaining to Turcios Lima should be there. What tricks of time and space should have taken *me* there, on the other hand, to find this relative hiding in an archive in New Haven, Connecticut, is the bigger mystery. His sister lives in Havana, often appearing on Spanish-language radio to tell their story. His story also appears in Roxanne Dunbar-Ortiz's "war years" memoir, *Outlaw Woman*, contextualized alongside the Women's Liberation Movement, the Vietnam War, the Weather Underground, the Civil Rights Movement, the African National Congress, and the American Indian Movement. Revolutionary Cuban artist and graphic designer Alfredo Rostgaard designed the cover of the book from which I adapted and lineated the above passage.

13 The investigative journalist is David Grann and I draw here on his *New Yorker* essay, "A Murder Foretold" (2011). The U.N. official whom he quotes is unnamed in his piece.

13–14 The descent to the underworld is the oldest part of this book. It references a sequence in the *Popul Vuh* when the hero twins, Hunahpu and Xbalenque, descend to the underworld called Xibalba to accomplish a set of cosmic tasks, not unlike those of Hercules or Jason in Colchis. One of the tasks is that they have to spend a night in the underworld house of the death bats, which they do by hiding inside their blowguns. Impatient to see if the bats had passed, Hunahpu peeking from the barrel of the gun is decapitated by Camazotz. Some Tzotzil and Tzeltal Mayans say that, after the arrival of the European gods, the Mayan gods retreated to caves and sinkholes (called cenotes) that interconnect the highlands of Chiapas and Guatemala. As poet Ámbar Past puts it in her conversation with Tzotzil collaborators, Xalic Guzmán Bakbolom and Xpetra Ernandes, in these caves "is the setting for the mythical drama in which the Maya soul is a principal actor. In the Netherworld, death is transformed into life. Animal spirit companions and plumed serpents of ancient songs live within the Earth alongside the capricious Mayan gods and goddesses" (45, 54–55). The persistence of a Mayan underworld in the contemporary moment itself captures contemporary experience, whose total finality in a Mayan underworld defines life as such. If the gods are 'deep hanging out' in the cenotes of Central America, the surfaces that make that depth visible are only so many manifestations of these divinities of the Americas.

14 The earthquake of 1917 actually did cover the sky with darkness and decapitate Columbus's statue. Guatemalan Nobel Laureate Miguel Ángel Asturias remembers that ominous time in an interview with literary critic Günter Lorenz (1970): "Yes, at 10:25 PM of 25 December 1917, an earthquake destroyed my city. I remember seeing something like an immense cloud covering the moon. I was in a cellar, a hole in the ground or a cave, or something like that. Right then and there I wrote my first poem, a goodbye song to Guatemala. Later on I was really mad by the circumstances under which the rubble was removed and by the social injustice that became really apparent then."

Nahualli Without Organs

17 The US occupation of Nicaragua is the common feature of our so-called 'singular modernity,' that is, the wars to control farmlands. In Nicaragua the situation was aggravated by US interest in maintaining sole control over a proposed Nicaraguan canal between the Atlantic and Pacific oceans. The canal has not been constructed. It might be the case that this is because the canal itself is not structurally viable. But another reason for its holdup might have to do with the spirit of rebellion to resist modernity's imposed singularity—famously summoned by the guerrilla Augusto César Sandino who beat back the US Marines between 1927 and 1933—which later was crystallized in the Sandinista government (FSLN) that ruled the country from 1979 to 1990. This part of their story is related to my story as well. It was the sale of crack cocaine in poor (and mostly black and brown) neighborhoods in the US that helped the CIA to found the counterrevolutionary guerrilla forces (the Contras). In my story, I draw on investigative journalist Gary Webb's famous work, *Dark Alliance*, which brought to light the relations between the Contras, the CIA, and the distribution networks of crack cocaine in Los Angeles in the 1980s (when the Cold War merged into the drug war). That distribution fueled a mass incarceration project that, in turn, fostered the growth of such prison gangs as Mara Salvatrucha. A constant hobbyhorse of contemporary US immigration vitriol, this gang is the product of the architects of the drug war and the various organizations that have profited from that architecture.

Our uncle mentioned here had the tragic distinction of being one of the first people to die of AIDS-related complications in El Salvador. He contracted the disease in Los Angeles and, sensing that he was sick, returned to his country to make peace with his fate. His story from that point on is the familiar one of stigma and fear that appends to mass moral panic: he died in biohazard quarantine in a hospital in San Salvador. As I understand it, he was rather like a Salvadoran Robert Duncan, deeply interested in poetry, mystical literature, hermetic psychology, divination, and things occult. I think we would have had a lot to talk about, had he lived for me to meet him as an adult.

18 The K'iche' Mayan daykeeper Andrés Xiloj Peruch spoke these words to the Tedlocks (qtd. in *2000 Years of Mayan Literature* and the essay "Toward a Poetics of Polyphony and Translatability"). For my understanding of Mesoamerican space-time, I draw on two books by the Tedlocks: Dennis's introduction to his magisterial translation of the Mayan *Popol Vuh* (1996) and Barbara's classic work on multi-metrical Mayan conceptions of space-time (its multi-temporality), *Time and the Highland Maya* ([1982] 1992), in addition to an essay that they co-authored in 1985, "Text and Textile: Language and Technology in the Arts of the Quiché Maya." Also, I quote James Maffie's philosophical achievement, *Aztec Philosophy: Understanding a World in Motion* (2014). Dennis and Barbara were initiated in the practice of daykeeping, a process Dennis describes in his fictocritical book, *Breath on the Mirror*. A daykeeper is a diviner of dreams and the Mayan calendric system, tracking the meanings of time's movement from one divinity's hands to the next (each day is a god in Mayan time; the handing over of time takes place at night, in the phantasmagoria of dreams), while performing the necessary rites to appease and celebrate these gods. Daykeepers must become skilled in mathematics, astronomy, botany, mineralogy, mythology, and calendrics to do their work, which typically involves the care and healing of individuals and communities.

19 In keeping with the poetry of sacred pairs, this collaborator won the Omnidawn book prize for poetry (for his book, *Place-Discipline*) the same year that I won the Fence Modern Poets Series. As this year contorts its violent but sobering eye, I have been thinking about its resonance (or what poet and anthropologist Susan Lepselter might call its "apophenia") in various anniversaries: the 30th anniversary of James Clifford's *The Predicament of Culture* (with its important essay "On Ethnographic Surrealism"), the 50th anniversary of the publication of Malinowski's diaries (an event through which the discipline of anthropology discovered its subconscious), the 50th anniversary of the protests of 1968, the 90th anniversary of the publication of Mariátegui's *Seven Interpretive Essays*, the 100th anniversary of the Russian Revolution, the 170th anniversary of the European revolutions of 1848, all reaching back to the 200th anniversary of the twin births of Karl Marx and Mary Shelley's *Frankenstein*. Moctezuma and I met at a community college in Southern California, when we were sixteen or so years old, and our mutual passion for poetry, as well as our autodidactism, brought us close. Since that time, we have worked together on many projects. The image of the stele superimposed with his poetry was from a chapbook project of which only a few cover ideas ever materialized. As Maffie notes, the technical term in Nahuatl for interdependent pairs is "inamic." With Moctezuma, I am inamic: complemented in collaboration with this old friend.

18 The Tzotzil Mayan word for nahualli is wayhel, which—Ámbar Past notes—is closely associated with dreams: "In addition to her soul, each person has an animal companion called a *wayhel*, a word grown from the root (*way*) of the verbs *to sleep* and *to dream*, and associated with shamanism, the portals to the Underworld, communication between the gods and the dead. The *wayhel* accompanies its alter ego from the moment it is born and may be a jaguar, a hawk, a hummingbird, a butterfly, a weasel, a caterpillar, or a water snake. Instead of a head, it may have an ax, a machete, a pair of scissors or even a cast-iron skillet stuck on the end of its neck. Witches may possess several *wayhel*: whirlwinds, rainbows, lightning bolts, and shooting stars. One of the most powerful forms of wayhel is the Writer, the *Scribanó*. This kind of *wayhel* is immortal because even after death she can recreate herself through marks on a piece of paper, or, as Pedro Pitarch explains: '... they invent themselves, writing themselves into existence.' The soul companions live with the Fathermothers in the heart of the mountain, sitting on the thirteen levels of bleachers inside the Earth. There the *wayhel* have radios, jukeboxes, even computers and e-mail. In dreams, the *wayhel* souls escape like naughty children and run around loose in the woods. If anything happens to her wayhel, a person will become ill. In these times when men are blasting new roads with dynamite, the earth trembles and the *wayhel* are afraid and can even die. A bad person may capture a *wayhel* and sell it to the Lord of the Cave, as happened to poor Maruch Vet. The soul is held captive in the way prisoners of war were held in ancient Mayan times, chained or tied with ropes awaiting sacrifice. The *wayhel* loses its appetite and becomes ill; its owner also gets sick. The seer offers a black hen to the cave so it will give back the stolen *wayhel* before her patient dies" (34–35).

20–21 I do not know who took the photograph, or who any of the swimmers in the water are. All I know is that the two women are my grandmother and her sister. And the log on which they balance hangs over the Gulf of Fonseca between Nicaragua and El Salvador.

Ohmaxac Packs

34 The quote from Apollonius of Rhodes (3rd century BCE) appears in the fourth book of his *Argonautica*, beginning at line 659, translated by R.C. Seaton (1912): "And here they found Circe bathing her head in the salt sea-spray, for sorely had she been scared by visions of the night. With blood her chambers and all the walls of her palace seemed to be running, and flame was devouring all the magic herbs with which she used to bewitch strangers whoever came; and she herself with murderous blood quenched the glowing flame, drawing it up in her hands; and she ceased from deadly fear. Wherefore when morning came she rose, and with sea-spray was bathing her hair and her garments. And beasts, not resembling the beasts of the wild, nor yet like men in body, but with a medley of limbs, went in a throng, as sheep from the fold in multitudes follow the shepherd. Such creatures, compacted of various limbs, did each herself produce from the primeval slime when she had not yet grown solid beneath a rainless sky nor yet had received a drop of moisture from the rays of the scorching sun; but time combined these forms and marshalled them in their ranks; in such wise these monsters shapeless of form followed her. And exceeding wonder seized the heroes, and at once, as each gazed on the form and face of Circe, they readily guessed that she was the sister of Aeetes." Apollonius's book is a conceptual template for the book in the reader's hands, and more broadly resonant with books that combine poetic, scholarly, and critical practices. The *Argonautica* was an epic written in a time of lyric poetry, evolving its landscape of thought and feeling from research in ethnography, literary studies, and comparative religious studies, while also a document of the intercultural ferment and temporal heterogeneity that was Ptolemaic Egypt (Apollonius was a librarian at the ancient Library of Alexandria). My comparison of Circe's magical staff to the staff of Hermes the Magician Trickster draws on observations made in Freudo-Marxist classicist Norman O. Brown's first book, *Hermes the Thief: The Evolution of a Myth* ([1947] 1990: 16). Comparably, in his quest to comprehend the implication of dreams, myths, and names in waking reality (i.e. to define a living ecology of dreams), Freudian anthropologist Géza Róheim identified Hermes as "the god of dreamland... the god of transitions," in as much as that this god of language, boundaries, and acts of exchange gives definition to "the episodes of myth in which a place is named after a certain event, and those in which a feature of the landscape originates in the body or in part of the body of a human being, merge into each other with imperceptible transitions" (11, 215).

The cited passages from Sahagún's *General History of the Things of New Spain* or the Florentine Codex (translated by Arthur J.O. Anderson and Charles E. Dibble) are in book two, chapter twelve, "On the fifteenth day of this month the young men and boys strewed boughs on all the altars and shrines of the gods, both those of which were in the houses and those which were along the roads and crossroads. And for this activity which they performed they gave them maize"; book three, chapter two, "And Titlacauan [Tezcatlipoca], who extended everywhere, was here therefore besought, prayed to, cried out to. And everywhere they set up his watching place, the mound, by the road, at crossroads"; book four, chapters eleven and twenty one: "When this [day came], everywhere in the Goddesses' sanctuaries and temples—everywhere offerings were made. For in every single place stood a temple of Goddesses, in each neighborhood, there at the crossroads. They covered with white streamers each of the images which were there—five [figures] of stone, placed in a row, their faces rubbed and painted with liquid rubber. He who made a vow to them covered them at the time of their descent, at the time of their day count, on the day sign of their descent. As many of them as there were he covered with white paper streamers" and "And so did they bury [a deceased woman who had been cursed], not at her home, but only leaving her there in the road; there at the very crossroads they buried her. They went skirmishing, fighting over her, and howling as they carried her. And as they brought her out of her house, it was not from the front; only at the back of the house, they broke a hole, through which they removed her so that they could leave her at the crossroads"; book five, chapter eight, "in which is told the omen which all took as a portent when they saw the chafer. Likewise all regarded as an omen the chafer, [which was] like a bright, brilliant red spider. When it entered someone's house, and he saw it, or he intercepted it on the road, they said: 'Now cometh sickness'; or, 'Now we will meet some [evil].' Perhaps now someone would chide him—something would shame him. And when it was seen in one's house, he who saw it forthwith seized it. He traced lines on the ground in the four directions: he made marks on the ground which he caused to take the form of a cross. And in the middle, at its center, he placed [the chafer] and there spat upon it. Thereupon he exhorted it; he said to it: 'Wherefore didsnt thou come? Let me see, [that] I may hasten to marvel at it!' Then he placed himself facing and looked toward the direction in which it would proceed. If now it went northward, thus he who looked knew that soon he was to die. But if it did not go toward there, thereby he knew that perchance it meant something [else] perhaps of no great consequence. He who was shown the omen said: 'Let it do [what it will]; let the little insect be aspersed! Shall we none the less be involved with it? Shall we none the less go with it? Later let us know what it meaneth.' The he seized it and left it at a crossroads. And some only threaded it on a hair and hung it up. If at dawn they saw that it no longer was there, they were then filled with much dread. But if it dawned and it hung at this very same place, they were consoled thereby. Little did they think of it; as nothing did they esteem it. And when they placed it in the midst of spittle or wine, they said it was made drunk by it. And also it was stated that sometime it spoke in two [ways]: it also boded good. Perhaps something fortunate would be one's reward."

Exceeding its ethnographic content, the form of Sahagún's book gives voice to the heterogeneous temporalities whose incommensurability surges with political (especially decolonial) possibilities. The paradoxical idea that a work of colonial ethnography could bear the forms through which decoloniality could happen is a constant theme of the present book. In its theorization of that theme, it draws on the works of political theorist Massimiliano Tomba, whose Walter Benjamin-inspired studies of temporal contradiction suggest that when time-scales do not match up in a process of production (for instance, when forms of subsistence farming, craftworks, religious devotion, music, poetry, etc. continue to structure a person's experience of time, amidst the efforts of capitalist production to totally dominate that time), they create non-synthesizing, politically tensioned breaks in a rhythm of social life. These tensions in the experience of time challenge the idea of an inherently dominant temporality (ecclesiastical, colonial, capitalist, or otherwise). All levels of antagonism are adequate for resisting subordination, and make wholes that we might call natures, worlds, organisms, or juridical and political reality. In my thinking about the poetics of such political arrhythmia, I have been helped as well by Marisol de la Cadena's book *Earth Beings* and the writings of Benjamin, Kathleen Stewart, and Cecilia Vicuña.

35 Hoffman and I came to-gether because of a shared interest in decolonizing sightlines. Putting ideas into practice, we developed our fictional ethnography in a variety of media, including painting, sculpture, collage, film, and writing. The touch-stone of our collaboration was her creation of a thir-ty-foot woven sculpture, like a bridge woven for disjoined worlds, which she installed  in the section of the Yale University Art Gallery dedicated to Indo-Pacific Art. Her background is from the Philippines and her work explores this trans-Pacific web, as it does in the above images where the weaving reaches to the statue of the Ifugao Bulul but stops short at the glass of the display case. In the middle image, she flips the paradigm of the museum on its head, transposing the picture that is here on the left into a display case held high in her sky-scape.

The book by Theodor de Bry which Hoffman creatively appropriates is his *Collectiones Peregrinatorium in Indiam Orientalem et Indiam Occidentalem* (1592), which disseminated images of the Americas as a cannibal free-for-all. From this strange stew, the Venusian "Book of Textures" recovers patterns of physical emplotment, or habitus, for a multi-temporal narrative weaving around the Star of Venus, whose significance for the native Americas is extensively documented. Regarding this Venusian "Book of Textures," I should note that the

Venusians were also known as the Big Star people, and their primary symbol was a serpent surrounded by seashells. The serpent represented their home planet and the seashells specified the coordinates for returning there. Its association with Venus can probably be attributed to the fact that, when this planet dances upon the waters of our planet's oceans (looking westward), its reflection assumes a light not unlike a snake with brilliant scales. While concrete evidence of the link to Venus has not been provided—it may be that the true meaning of their symbolism will never be known—most often, the symbol appears on their quilts of deep blue intersected with orange and silver thread.

Journaling

40 The partially omitted name that precedes the break in syntactic "sense" is that of a childhood friend who died in hard circumstances. After a car crash left him partially paralyzed, he took his life in front of a police station. A poem by William Blake crystallizes the experience of seeing a lost friend in a dream: "O what Land is the Land of Dreams / What are its Mountains & what are its Streams... // But tho calm & warm the Waters wide / I could not get to the other side... // The Land of Dreams is better far/Above the light of the Morning Star" (486–87). Dreams crumble into the "emotional force" of a situation, to quote Renato Rosaldo, creating those "myriad crossroads and borderlands" by which we pick apart the contradictions of our dreams. Another "tender cocoon suspended in the dream world... as if the conditions and possibilities of a life have themselves begun to float," quoting Kathleen Stewart now (61), another fracturing of the archive into the reckless redemption of connections (an effort akin to Lévi-Strauss's *efflorescence passagère*).

Diary in the Strict Sense

45 As the third installment of this "Diary in the Strict Sense" tells (pg. 78), these entries are reworked versions of Bronislaw Malinowksi's diary entries in the Western Pacific. I appropriate the diary whose publication in 1968 famously upended the discipline of anthropology, because that upending revealed something of the *traumzeit* in ethnographic writing. Malinowski is celebrated as the first anthropologist to advocate fieldwork, engagement with native people, and dialogic understandings of foreign societies and cultures. In this regard, he was one of the first modernist social anthropologists, breaking with Victorian anthropological frameworks of "armchair" analogy (of which Frazer's *Golden Bough* is the most famous example). Malinowski's *Argonauts of the Western Pacific* (1922) and *Coral Gardens and their Magic* (1935) are achievements of ethnography, theory, description, and real poetry. He wished to be the Joseph Conrad of anthropology.

But—as James Clifford, George Stocking, and others noted—the diaries revealed that he had the Kurtz of Conrad's *Heart of Darkness* in him too: paranoia, racism, jealousy, lust, hatred, anger, instability, violence, and obsession are the hallmark themes of these private writings made public. They show an ethnographer in the field "alone with his instincts" (Stocking), but whose instincts root in darkest passion. In the controversy that ensued from their publication, anthropology discovered its sordid disciplinary subconscious. More than any other book, then, this is an instance of what Clifford termed "ethnographic surrealism." In my own engagement with the colonial *traumlandschaft*, it was only appropriate to appropriate its foundational words, images, themes, and energies, traduced in this other landscape, the originary mytheme of Colón; but it also twisted into the anthropological subconscious writhing in Malinowski's writings.

Journaling

49 This is a collage that builds on the first (pg. 3) by splicing a comics version of Edgar Rice Burroughs's Tarzan character with an encyclopedia entry about fakirs in Nepal (a child [pretending to be?] dead with an abundance of weird dignity) and, more generally, rites for the dead.

58 This collage, also my work, inverts cutouts of Yaqui deer dancers over a scene painted by the television personality Bob Ross. The idea is to evoke, once again, Blake's rebel-savior Satan in the shadows of our collapsing, softly televisual, hearing-voices worlds. The world here is presented similarly to how it is in the collage of page 43, in which the encyclopedia entry is the material inverse of the cutout cartouche—an illuminated letter by the fifteenth-century Italian miniaturist Giovanni Gadio—that depicts the ascension of the collage on page 3. Another way of thinking about the cartouche is as a talking box, or television, which is suggested in some accounts of Mayan political discourse. In 1867, a box that held three talking stones (sometimes said to have been a talking cross) led a rebellion of Mayan peasants in the Caste War of Yucatán. Likewise, in the wake of the so-called postmodern Zapatista uprising, a talking box emerged in the mountains of San Cristóbal de las Casas in Chiapas: "the voice from the talking box of María Ernándes Kokov, a modern commercialized version of a Mayan oracle, was taped in 1996 during an eclipse of the Moon seen from her house up on the Huitepec Mountain, in between the antennas of Televisión Azteca and a traditional animist shrine. The Saint, named Pagresito, 'Little Daddy,' spoke with a falsetto voice to his keeper... who calls herself the Defender of the Angels" (Past 38). Blake enfolded: "Once a dream did weave a shade/O'er my Angel-guarded bed" (16).

Bowl-Maker

59 The anthropological work quoted here is Marshall Sahlins's *What Kinship Is—And Is Not*. Interlocked in his lifelong study of the relationship between structure and event, the proper context for his conception of kinship is the play between semiosis and poetics. As he puts it, theories about structure and event regularly exaggerate the distinction between the two: "the event [is] conceived as antistructural, the structure as nullifying the event." Such exaggeration leads to a range of dubious dialectic negations: "structure is to event [i.e. mutually negating] as the social to the individual, the invisible to the visible, the lawful to the aleatory, the quotidian to the extraordinary, the silent to the audible, the anonymous to the authored, the normal to the traumatic, the comparable to the unique, and so on" ([1991] 2000: 294, 295–6); yielding a table of oppositions to which poets might add, the formal to the contextual, the written to the oral, the poetic to the pragmatic, the mediated to the spontaneous, the technology to the technique, the measure to the excess, the global to the local, and so on. Theories about structural flatness or evenemental unwieldiness are stopgaps because in practice the opposition between structure and event is not one of mutual exclusion; it is reciprocal and dynamic, semiotic and aesthetic. Cultural structures modulate events that provide the occasions for cultural structures to modulate events, and so on: "the claim is not that culture determines history, only that it organizes it" (2004: 11). It is likewise for the relation between cultural and genetic kinship, each lurking in the disclosures of the other. And the same goes for the relation between poetics and the activities of a dream, the animating principle of the book in the reader's hands being that the former organizes the latter's organizing force: it is a study about how language is captivated by and captures the negativity of the hemispheric experience surging from its southern sources. **Photograph of Bowl Maker on pg. 68 by Carolyn Chema.**

Diary in the Strict Sense

70 For Malinowski, to go "South" from the coral atolls around New Guinea would have meant to return to Australia. Róheim's contemporaneous anthropological work on the aboriginal cultures of Australia was most deeply engaged with the concept of "*altjirerinja*" or "alcheringa" as the famous ethnopoetics journal of the 1970s and 80s transliterated it. This word means the "dreaming" or dreamtime in which ancestors, myth, ritual, history, and present humans and nonhumans meet in "imperceptible transitions"; "intertribal mythological paths," Róheim also described it, while admitting that the concept confused him. As Tedlock suggests with his conception of "mythistory" (see next note), what frustrated Róheim is his desire to keep the reality principle clean or pure of myth and dreams: Róheim is averse to the idea of "rehistoricizing" in the dream and allowing the tradition to be "redreamt"—that is, the idea that "*es hat mir getraumt* (it dreamt itself to me)" could be possible. "The question is whether we are dealing with history or fantasy. In various Australian languages we find identical or similar words for dream, the mythical past, and ancestors. Are these narratives based on dreams? or how are we to interpret this identity of names?" (6–7, 210). Interestingly, the problem of the dreaming becomes an instance in which Róheim encounters his own set of Freudian themes and mythemes (this is before Lévi-Strauss): he describes these historical, oneiric, and ritual elements as "abreacting" to one another, showing themselves in "pantomime." An idea constellates here between emotion, gesture, dream, and historicity that—maybe—could only be called "alcheringa." Tedlock (who co-edited that journal) wrote a book of calendric dream poetry based on a Mayan system of dream interpretation (the daykeeping), *Days from a Dream Almanac*. It emphasizes that, once you release yourself to the dreamtime, there is no stopping its workings inside you and you inside it; when you stir those signs you elicit their rhythms, which will affect the way you move: "What is sought is the sheet lightning that moves silently over distant horizons, where dark lakes stir with reflected flickers. When this kind of lightning comes close, it moves silently over the horizons of the daykeeper's body, stirring the blood... Like the struggle with dreams, the sensing and reading of lightning in the blood is not something that can simply be put aside when one comes out of the field, to be summoned up only when one chooses to write about it. It makes the entire body into a thinking instrument, and although counting the days or talking or writing about the blood makes the lightning more likely to stir, there is no way, short of getting completely exhausted or hopelessly drunk, to prevent it from moving. It is like a quiet second mind, always ready to tap the noisy mind on the shoulder" (xiii–xiv).

78 Here I integrate pieces and threads of Malinowski's diary into the structure of what Dennis Tedlock called "mythistory," which was his way of describing time in Mayan cosmology. Rather than unilear progress (or static circularity), Mayan time is comprised of an intersection of threads of which each represents different temporalities: mythic, human, animal, mineral, and so on. Because these threads intersect, like a weaving or mat, any pressure or movement on a thread affects the whole structure of time (pulls in the time-thread of the gods affect human experience, as much as pulls in the time-threads of humans affect the experiences of the gods). The threads are "interpenetrating rather than mutually exclusive." In his introduction to the *Popol Vuh*, he writes: "We tend to think of myth and history as being in conflict with each other, but the authors of the inscriptions at Palenque and the alphabetical text of the *Popol Vuh* treated the mythic and historical parts of their narratives as belonging to a single, balanced whole... For Mayans, the presence of a divine dimension in narratives of human affairs is not an imperfection but a necessity, and it is balanced by a necessary human dimension in narratives of divine affairs. At one end of the *Popol Vuh* the gods are preoccupied with the difficult task of making humans, and at the other humans are preoccupied with the equally difficult task of finding the traces of divine movements in their deeds" (58–59). In practical terms, this is instanced in his ethnography of myth and magic, *Breath on the Mirror*, as a fictocritical mode in which the author slips into the worlds, objects, relations, and events he sets out to describe. Every part is adequate to the whole, each whole tessellating its folding parts; so that, eventually, you see the gods and other beings of myth wearing backpacks while you end up with the tumpline over your head. He tells us that the K'iche' term for this way of thinking is "*kajulew* or "'sky-earth' [which] preserves the duality of what we call the 'world.'" By duality he means, in addition to a table of inter-animating oppositions (sky/earth, hot/cold, rain/stones, etc.), the interpenetration of experience and its exposition; or the way in which, if you study the signs of the Americas, they will shape and condition the framework in which you study them.

Journaling

85 We took this photograph (drawing here by Serin Lee) on our visit to the museum of anthropology (Museo Nacional de Antropología) in San Salvador. In it, the clay figure of a warrior wears the skin of the animal. With this book, I wear the skins of Columbus.

Oneirography

Adès, Dawn and Simon Baker. *Undercover Surrealism: Georges Bataille and DOCUMENTS*. The MIT Press, 2006.

Adorno, Theodor. *Dream Notes*. Translated by Rodney Livingstone, Polity Press, 2007.

———. *Minima Moralia: Reflections on a Damaged Life*. Translated by E. F. N Jephcott, Verso, 2005.

Anaya, Rudolfo. *A Chicano in China*. U of New Mexico P, 1986.

Anzaldúa, Gloria. *Light in the Dark/Luz en lo Oscuro*. Edited by AnaLouise Keating. Duke UP, 2015.

Artís-Gener, Avel·lí. *Palabras de Opoton el Viejo: Crónica Mexicana del Siglo XVI*. Siglo XXI, 1992.

Asturias, Miguel Ángel and Gunter W. Lorenz. "Miguel Ángel Asturias with Gunter W. Lorenz." *Review*, no. 15, pp. 5–11.

Benjamin, Walter. "Diary from August 7, 1931, to the Day of My Death." *Selected Writings, Vol. 2, No. 2, 1931–1934*, edited by Michael Jennings, Howard Eiland, and Gary Smith, translated by Rodney Livingstone, Harvard UP, 2005, pp. 501–506.

———. "Dream Kitsch." *Walter Benjamin's Archive*, edited by Ursula Marx, Gudrun Schwarz, Michael Schwarz, and Erdmut Wizila, translated by Esther Leslie, Verso, 2015, fig. 3.4.

———. *The Origin of German Tragic Drama*, translated by John Osborne, Verso, 2009.

Berger, John. *And Our Faces, My Heart, Brief as Photos*. Vintage, 1984.

Blake, William. *The Complete Poetry and Prose of William Blake*. Edited by David Erdman. Anchor, 1982.

———. *The Drawings for Dante's Divine Comedy*. Edited by Sebastien Schütze and Maria Antonietta Terzoli. Taschen, 2014.

Brown, Norman O. *Hermes the Thief: The Evolution of a Myth*. U of Wisconsin P, 1947.

———. *Love's Body*. Random House, 1966.

Césaire, Aimé. "Keeping Poetry Alive," translated by Connie Rosemont, in *Black, Brown, and Beige: Surrealist Writings from Africa and the Diaspora*, edited by Franklin Rosemont and Robin D.G. Kelley, U of Texas P, 2009, pp. 77–78.

Chakrabarty, Dipesh. *Provincializing Europe: Postcolonial Thought and Historical Difference*. Princeton UP, 2000.

Clifford, James. "On Ethnographic Surrealism." *The Predicament of Culture: Twentieth-Century Ethnography, Literature, and Art*. Harvard UP, 1988, pp. 117–151.

de Bry, Theodor. *Collectiones Peregrinatorium in Indiam Orientalem et Indiam Occidentalem*. 1592.

de la Cadena, Marisol. *Earth Beings: Ecologies of Practice Across Andean Worlds.* Duke UP, 2016.

de las Casas, Bartolomé. *The Journal of Christopher Columbus,* translated by Cecil Jane, Clarkson N. Potter, 1960.

Deleuze, Gilles. "What is an Event?" *The Fold: Leibniz and the Baroque,* translated by Tom Conley, U of Minnesota P, 1993, pp. 76–82.

Documents: Doctrines, Archéologie, Beaux-Arts, Ethnographie, Varietiés. Années 1929 et 1930. Editions Jean-Michel Place, 1991.

Dunbar-Ortiz, Roxanne. *An Indigenous Peoples' History of the United States.* Beacon P, 2015

———. *Outlaw Woman: A Memoir of the War Years, 1960–1975.* U of Oklahoma P, 2014.

Friedrich, Paul. *The Language Parallax: Linguistic Relativism and Poetic Indeterminacy.* U of Texas P, 1986.

Galeano, Eduardo. *Guatemala: Occupied Country.* Monthly Review, 1968.

Garfield, Patricia. *Creative Dreaming.* Ballantine, 1974.

The Golden Fleece: Tales from the Caucasus (The Georgian, Armenian, and Azerbaijanian Magic Tales). Translated by Avril Pyman, Progress Publishers, 1971.

Grann, David. "A Murder Foretold." *The New Yorker,* April 4, 2011.

Guaman Poma de Ayala, Felipe. *Primer Nueva Corónica y Buen Govierno.* Det Kongelige Biblioteke, http://www.kb.dk/permalink/2006/poma/info/en/frontpage. htm, accessed May 5, 2018.

Guntarik, Olivia and Michael Angelo Tata. "Telematic Delta Waves: Philosophy as Oneirography." *New Writing,* 2019.

Horkheimer, Max and Theodor Adorno. "Excursus I: Odysseus or Myth and Enlightenment." *Dialectic of Enlightenment: Philosophical Fragments,* translated by Edmund Jephcott, Stanford UP, 2002, pp. 35–62.

Krämer, Michael. *El Salvador: Unicornio de la Memoria.* Ediciones Museo de la Palabra y la Imagen, 2009.

Lacan, Jacques. *Écrits: The First Complete Edition in English.* Translated by Bruce Fink, Norton, 2006.

Le Clézio, J. M. G. *The Mexican Dream: Or, the Interrupted Thought of Amerindian Civilizations.* Translated by Teresa Lavender Fagan, U of Chicago P, 1993.

Leiris, Michel. *Phantom Africa.* Translated by Brent Hayes Edwards, U of Chicago P, 2017.

León-Portilla, Miguel. *Time and Reality in the Thought of the Maya.* Translated by Charles Boilès and Fernando Horcasitas, Beacon P, 1973.

Lepselter, Susan. *The Resonance of Unseen Things: Poetics, Power, Captivity, and UFOs in the American Uncanny.* U of Michigan P, 2016.

Lévi-Strauss, Claude. *Tristes Tropiques.* Penguin Classics, 2012.

Lingis, Alphonso. "The Rapture of the Deep." *In Excesses: Eros and Culture.* SUNY Press, 1983, pp. 1–16.

Maffie, James. *Aztec Philosophy: Understanding a World in Motion.* UP of Colorado, 2014.

Malinowski, Bronislaw. *A Diary in the Strict Sense of the Term*. Stanford UP, 1989.

Mariátegui, José Carlos. *Seven Interpretive Essays on Peruvian Reality*. Translated by Marjory Urquidi. U of Texas P, [1928] 1988.

Martínez Parédez, Domingo. *El Popol Vuh Tiene Razon: Teoria Sobre la Cosmogonia Preamericana*. Editorial Orion, 1968.

McLean, Stuart. "Sea," in *Crumpled Paper Boat: Experiments in Ethnographic Writing*, edited by Anand Pandian and Stuart McLean, Duke UP, 2017, pp. 148–167.

Miller, Mary and Karl Taube. *The Gods and Symbols of Ancient Mexico and the Maya: An Illustrated Dictionary*. Thames and Hudson, 1993.

Montes, César. *Turcios Lima*. Tricontinental, 1968.

Morison, Samuel Eliot. "Texts and Translations of the Journal of Columbus's First Voyage." *The Hispanic American Historical Review*, vol. 19, no. 3, 1939, pp. 235–261.

Nietzsche, Friedrich. *The Gay Science*. Translated by Walter Kaufmann, Vintage Books, 1974.

———. *On The Advantage and Disadvantage of History for Life*. Translated by Peter Preuss, Hackett Classics, 1980.

Obarrio, Juan. "Postshamanism (1999)." *Cultural Studies Review*, vol. 13, no. 2, 2007, pp. 166–189.

Opie, Iona and Peter Opie. *The Lore and Language of Schoolchildren*. New York Review of Books Classics, 2000.

Olson, Charles. *The Maximus Poems*. U of California P, 1985.

Past, Ámbar, *Xalic Guzmán Bakbolom, and Xpetra Ernandes. Incantations: Songs, Spells, and Images by Mayan Women*. Cinco Puntos P, 2005.

Paz, Octavio. *The Monkey Grammarian*. Translated by Helen Lane, Arcade, 2017.

Pietz, William. "The Problem of the Fetish, I." *RES: Anthropology and Aesthetics*, no. 9, 1985, pp. 5–17.

Pound, Ezra. *The Cantos*. New Directions, 1970.

Rankine, Claudia. *Citizen: An American Lyric*. Graywolf Press, 2014.

Rhodius, Apollonius. *Argonautica*. Translated by Robert Seaton, Harvard UP, 1912.

Ricoeur, Paul. *Memory, History, Forgetting*. Translated by Kathleen Blamey and David Pellauer, U of Chicago P, 2004.

Róheim, Géza. *The Eternal Ones of the Dream: A Psychoanalytic Interpretation of Australian Myth and Ritual*. International Universities P, 1945.

Rosaldo, Renato. *Culture and Truth: The Remaking of Social Analysis*. Beacon, 1989.

———. *The Day of Shelly's Death: The Poetry and Ethnography of Grief*. Duke UP, 2013.

Sahagún, Bernardino de. *Florentine Codex: General History of the Things of New Spain*. Translated by Arthur J.O. Anderson and Charles E. Dibble, U of Utah P, 2012.

Sahlins, Marshall. *Apologies to Thucydides: Understanding History as Culture and Vice Versa*. U of Chicago P, 2004.

———. "The Return of the Event, Again." *Culture in Practice: Selected Essays*. Zone Books, 2000, pp. 293–352.

———. *What Kinship Is—And Is Not*. U of Chicago P, 2014.

Sanjinés, Javier. *Embers of the Past: Essays in Times of Decolonization*. Translated by David Frye, Duke UP, 2013.

Sebald, W.G. *The Emigrants*. Translated by Michael Hulse. New Directions, 1997.

———. *The Rings of Saturn*. Translated by Michael Hulse. New Directions, 1999.

Stedman, John Gabriel. *Narrative of a Five Years Expedition against the Revolted Negroes of Surinam*. Edited by Richard Price and Sally Price, Open Road, 2016.

Stevenson, Lisa. "A Proper Message," in *Crumpled Paper Boat: Experiments in Ethnographic Writing*, edited by Anand Pandian and Stuart McLean, Duke UP, 2017, pp. 209–221.

Stewart, Kathleen. *Ordinary Affects*. Duke UP, 2007.

———. "Writing, Life." *PMLA*, vol. 133, no. 1, 2018, pp. 186–189.

Taussig, Michael. *The Magic of the State*. Routledge, 1997.

———. *Shamanism, Colonialism, and the Wild Man: A Study in Terror and Healing*. U of Chicago P, 1987.

———. "Viscerality, Faith, and Skepticism: Another Theory of Magic." *Hau: Journal of Ethnographic Theory*, vol. 6, no. 3, 2016, pp. 453–483.

Tedlock, Barbara. *Time and the Highland Maya*. U of New Mexico P, 1992.

——— and Dennis Tedlock. "Text and Textile: Language and Technology in the Arts of the Quiché Maya. *Journal of Anthropological Research*, vol. 41, no. 2, 1985, pp. 121–146.

Tedlock, Dennis. 2000 Years of Mayan Literature. U of California P, 2010.

———. *Breath on the Mirror: Mythic Voices and Visions of the Living Maya*. HarperCollins, 1993.

———. *Days from a Dream Almanac*. U of Illinois P, 1999.

———. "Drawing and Designing with Words." *Parallel Worlds: Genre, Discourse, and Poetics in Contemporary, Colonial, and Classic Period Maya Literature*, edited by Kerry M. Hull and Michael D. Carrasco, UP of Colorado, 2012, pp. 181–194.

———, trans. *Popol Vuh: The Definitive Edition of the Mayan Book of Dawn of Life and the Glories of Gods and Kings*. Simon and Schuster, 1996.

———. "Toward a Poetics of Polyphony and Translatability." *Close Listening: Poetry and the Performed Word*, edited by Charles Bernstein, Oxford UP, 1998, pp. 178–199.

Tomba, Massimiliano. *Marx's Temporalities*. Translated by Peter Thomas and Sara Farris, Haymarket, 2013.

Vicuña, Cecilia. *Saborami*. ChainLinks, [1973] 2011.

———. *Unravelling Words and the Weaving of Water*. Graywolf Press, 1992.

Vizenor, Gerald. *The Heirs of Columbus*. Wesleyan UP, 1991.

Wagner, Roy. *Symbols that Stand for Themselves*. U of Chicago P, 1986.

Webb, Gary. *Dark Alliance: The CIA, the Contras, and the Crack Cocaine Explosion*. Seven Stories P, 1999.

Wynter, Sylvia. "Columbus, the Ocean Blue, and Fables that Stir the Mind: To Reinvent the Study of Letters." *Poetics of the Americas: Race, Founding, Textuality*, edited by Bainard Cowan and Jefferson Humphries, Louisiana State UP, 1997, pp. 141–163.

Yates, Frances. *The Art of Memory*. Routledge, 1966.

Zavaleta Mercado, René. *Towards a History of the National-Popular in Bolivia, 1879–1980*. Translated by Anne Freeland, Seagull Books, 2018.

Acknowledgments

This book benefitted from its interactions with Elizabeth Ault, James Chandler, Ramón Gutierrez, Roberto Harrison, Camille Hoffman, Jose-Luis Moctezuma, Barbara Mor, Fred Moten, Juan Obarrio, Ariana Reines, Zachary Samalin, Michael Taussig, Christopher Taylor, Dennis Tedlock, Rachel Thompson, Rodrigo Toscano, Cecilia Vicuña, and John Wilkinson. In close conversation with its ideas from the outset, and at every step of the book's growth, Srikanth Reddy deserves special thanks. I am grateful to have found in Rebecca Wolff an editor with poetic vision to match intellectual care. Two anonymous reviewers gave me maps to the colonial dreamlands—maps that I did not know existed, which helped me immensely as I crossed and re-crossed these lands. I am probably guilty of having spoken too much about this book's ideas in a graduate seminar on "Anthropological Poetics" at the University of Chicago. To the wonderful students of that class: my apologies, but thank you.

The project also grew in conversations made possible by the Institute for Critical Social Inquiry at The New School, as well as the Provost's Postdoctoral Fellows Program and the Neubauer Family Assistant Professor Program at the University of Chicago.

My gratitude to Alexis Chema, in whose arms the book dreamt itself, is deep beyond acknowledgment.